FUNNY & FABULOUS FRACTION STORIES

30 Reproducible Math Tales and Problems To Reinforce Important Fraction Skills

by Dan Greenberg

SCHOLASTIC
PROFESSIONAL BOOKS

New York · Toronto · London · Auckland · Sydney

Cover design by Jaime Lucero, Liza Charlesworth, and Vincent Ceci
Interior design by Robert Dominguez and Jaime Lucero for Grafica, Inc.
Illustrations by Jared Lee

ISBN 0-590-96576-X

Contents

HOW TO USE THIS BOOK **5**

THE BASICS

Skill 1: Picturing Fractions
Martha Crunch, Personal
Fractions Trainer **9**

Skill 2: Recognizing Fractions
Great Artists of the World
Draw Fractions **11**

Skill 3: Drawing and Identifying Fractions
The History of Fractions: A Play **13**

Skill 4: Comparing Fractions
Dear Ms. Fraction **16**

Skill 5: Equivalent Fractions
Louie Lewis, Fractional Private Eye . . **18**

Skill 6: Introduction To Simplest Form
Martha and Steve: Simplest Form . . **20**

Skill 7: Improper Fractions and Mixed Numbers
Joe Trella, Fraction Fella **22**

Skill 8: Practice Simplest Form
Never More, Baltimore! **25**

Skill Review
Ultra Workout 1 . . . . **27**

ADDING AND SUBTRACTING FRACTIONS

Skill 9: Adding and Subtracting Fractions with Like Denominators
Rex Roper's Believe It or Not! **28**

Skill 10: Adding and Subtracting Mixed Numbers with Like Denominators
Texarkana Bernstein: The World's
Greatest Adventurer and Her Trusty
Dog, Woovis (Episode 1) **31**

Skill 11: Least Common Denominators
Officer Meg O'Malley of the Fraction
Police **35**

Skill 12: Adding and Subtracting Fractions with Unlike Denominators
Martha's Brain **38**

Skill 13: Adding Mixed Numbers with Unlike Denominators
Texarkana Bernstein: The World's
Greatest Adventurer and Her Trusty
Dog, Woovis (Episode 2) **40**

Skill 14: Subtracting Mixed Numbers with Unlike Denominators
Billy Doogan, Roving Weather Man . . **43**

Skill Review
Ultra Workout, Too! **46**

continued on next page

Contents

MULTIPLYING AND DIVIDING FRACTIONS

Skill 15: Multiplying Fractions by Whole Numbers
Emily Taproot, Fractional Poet **47**

Skill 16: Multiplying Fractions
The Frackie Awards **49**

Skill 17: Reciprocals
Emily Taproot's Winky-Tinky
Tigglesworth **52**

Skill 18: Dividing Fractions
Louie Lewis: The Case of the
Flipping Fractions. **54**

Skill 19: Multiplying And Dividing Mixed Numbers
Officer Meg O'Malley: Episode 2 . . . . **56**

Skill 20: Multiplying and Dividing Mixed Numbers
Yucky Cooking with Mr. Pierre **58**

Skill 21: Multiplying and Dividing Fractions
Martha Crunch and Her Amazing
Fraction Workout Video **60**

Skill Review
Ultra Workout 3! **62**

USING FRACTIONS

Skill 22: Multiplying Probabilities
The Critics **63**

Skill 23: Ratios
Arnold Guck: Man or Myth? **65**

Skill 24: Equivalent Fractions and Decimals
Enid The Magnificent, Part 1 . . . . . . **68**

Skill 25: Equivalent Fractions and Decimals
Enid the Magnificent, Part 2:
Enid Does the Unthinkable. **70**

Skill 26: Fraction Number Sense
Name That Fraction **72**

Skill 27: Multiplication, Division and Addition
Martha's Brain Game **75**

TEST 1: THE ULTIMATE FRACTION WORKOUT, PART ONE. 77

TEST 2: THE ULTIMATE FRACTION WORKOUT, PART TWO 79

ANSWERS. 82

How To Use This Book

Welcome to *Funny & Fabulous Fraction Stories*!

Fractions are a tricky topic. Neither completely concrete or abstract, they mark the transition in math from the purely representational to the purely symbolic. Because of this, many students find fractions difficult to learn—and many teachers find them difficult to teach.

This book seeks to make fractions more accessible to both students and teachers by introducing an element of fun. The stories, poems, plays, and parodies contained in these pages are designed to entertain your students and at the same time to give them a solid grasp of important fractional concepts. The characters and situations in each activity will also help students apply the concepts they learn to real-life situations—a key element of the National Council of Teachers of Mathematics' Curriculum Standards.

The stories in this book are intended to appeal to all kinds of learners, including:

- students at all achievement levels
- students working with fractions for the first time
- older students who need review and enrichment
- students who find it difficult to visualize and conceptualize fractions
- students not easily motivated by traditional textbooks
- students who seek a connection between their own lives and mathematical concepts

THE BOOK'S COMPONENTS

THE ACTIVITIES
This book is divided into four sections:

- **The Basics**, which covers general fractional concepts, from visualizing fractions to expressing fractions in simplest form

- **Adding and Subtracting Fractions**

- **Multiplying and Dividing Fractions**

- **Using Fractions**, where students apply the fraction skills they have learned to calculate probability, ratios, and decimals.

Sprinkled throughout the book are a series of "One Way to Do It" tip boxes. Each suggests a strategy which students may find helpful in solving the problems in that particular activity. Students should not be limited to that specific solving strategy, however; if they prefer using a method other than the one suggested in the box, by all means encourage them to try it.

To make selecting appropriate activities an easier task, the table of contents lists the primary concepts covered in each activity.

ASSESSMENT
Each of the first three sections concludes with a Skill Workout that reinforces concepts covered in that section. In addition, two tests appear at the end of the book.

- Test No. 1 covers sections 1 and 2, including basic fraction concepts and addition and subtraction of fractions.

- Test No. 2 covers sections 3 and 4, including multiplication and division of fractions, reciprocals, ratios, and conversion of fractions to decimals.

THE SOLUTIONS
Annotated solutions to each of the 27 activities, plus the workouts and tests, are located on pages 82 to 88.

HOW THE ACTIVITIES CAN BE USED

The stories in this book can be used in a variety of ways.

- You can use the activities as a framework from which to approach fractions, or as a supplement to classroom activities.

- You can work through the problems in sequence, or reinforce skills as you see fit.

- Students can work on the stories individually, in teams or groups, or as a class.

- Stories can be assigned to students for independent self-paced study.

- Activities can be read as part of an interdisciplinary program that includes storytelling, fantasy, humor, or literature.

TEACHING TIPS

- The use of manipulatives is an excellent way to reinforce the skills presented in this book. For even more enrichment, have students brainstorm other real-life applications of the fraction concepts presented in each activity.

- Encourage students to explore different problem-solving methods when working on an activity. In addition, remind them that the best way to be sure they've done a problem correctly is to check their work.

- Many students find word problems like the ones in this book challenging. Make sure students carefully read the problems and are able to state the question being asked before they attempt to solve them.

- Present the activities in unique ways. If a story is written in dialogue form, for example, assign roles to students and have them read it aloud.

- Once students have shown an understanding of fractional concepts, allow them to use calculators to solve some of the more challenging word problems presented in the book.

I hope this book helps you to motivate your students to a greater understanding of fraction concepts. I know they'll have a great time learning them!

—DAN GREENBERG

Name

Martha Crunch, Personal Fractions Trainer

Hi. I'm Martha Crunch, your personal fractions trainer. And this is Steve. Say hello, Steve.

Ra-a-ah! Ee-e-urk!

Welcome to fractions, the Martha Crunch way.

You know what really gets me? People who think fractions are hard. Doing 250 jumping jacks on a gravel driveway—barefoot … now that's hard. Compared to that, fractions are a PIECE OF CAKE.

So what do you say? Are you ready to learn fractions…

…the Martha Crunch way?

Ra-a-ah! Ee-e-urk! When do we start?

Right now, Steve.

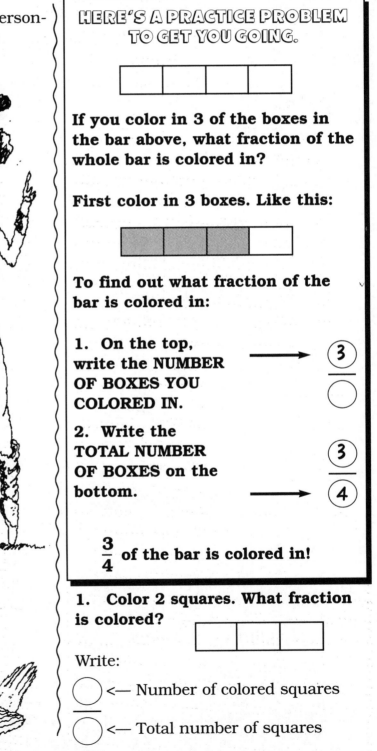

HERE'S A PRACTICE PROBLEM TO GET YOU GOING.

If you color in 3 of the boxes in the bar above, what fraction of the whole bar is colored in?

First color in 3 boxes. Like this:

To find out what fraction of the bar is colored in:

1. On the top, write the NUMBER OF BOXES YOU COLORED IN. → ③ / ◯

2. Write the TOTAL NUMBER OF BOXES on the bottom. → ③ / ④

$\frac{3}{4}$ of the bar is colored in!

1. Color 2 squares. What fraction is colored?

Write:

◯ <— Number of colored squares
—
◯ <— Total number of squares

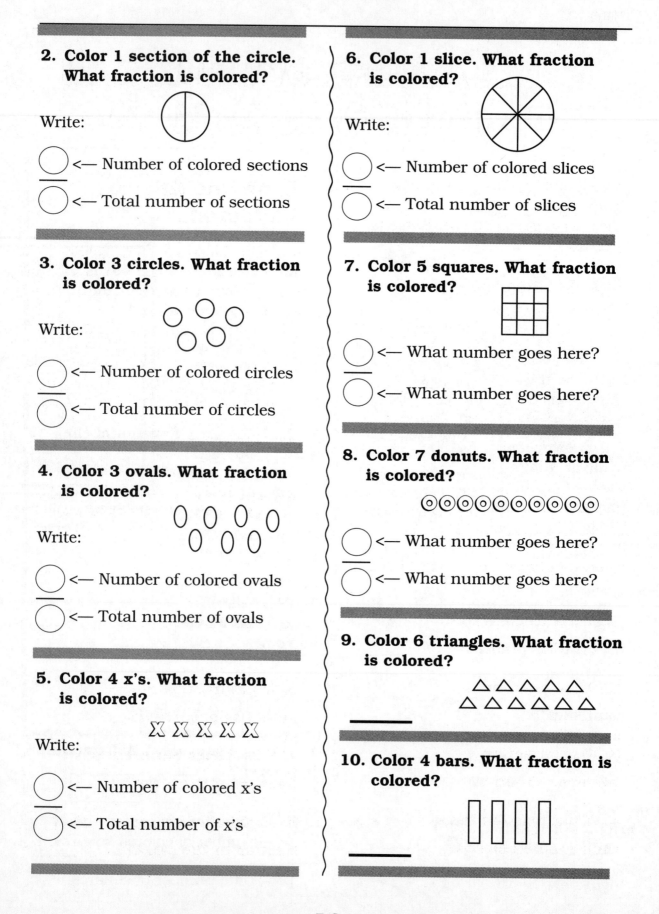

2. Color 1 section of the circle. What fraction is colored?

Write:

◯ <— Number of colored sections
—
◯ <— Total number of sections

3. Color 3 circles. What fraction is colored?

Write:

◯ <— Number of colored circles
—
◯ <— Total number of circles

4. Color 3 ovals. What fraction is colored?

Write:

◯ <— Number of colored ovals
—
◯ <— Total number of ovals

5. Color 4 x's. What fraction is colored?

X X X X X

Write:

◯ <— Number of colored x's
—
◯ <— Total number of x's

6. Color 1 slice. What fraction is colored?

Write:

◯ <— Number of colored slices
—
◯ <— Total number of slices

7. Color 5 squares. What fraction is colored?

◯ <— What number goes here?
—
◯ <— What number goes here?

8. Color 7 donuts. What fraction is colored?

◯ <— What number goes here?
—
◯ <— What number goes here?

9. Color 6 triangles. What fraction is colored?

10. Color 4 bars. What fraction is colored?

Name _____

Great Artists of the World Draw Fractions

Five of the world's great artists have volunteered to explain how their most famous work relates to fractions.

Pablo Pescado:

I paint fishes. Only fishes. Always fishes. People ask me, "Pablo, why fishes?" I say to them: Why not fishes? No one has ever been able to give me a reason why not. Can you?

Fishes, Fishes
by Pablo Pescado

Leonardo da Pepperoni:

Look into the eyes of the young woman. They tell a story. It is a love story. It is a story of a woman and a pizza. She loves the pizza because it has extra cheese. I hate to brag. But to me, this is the most beautiful painting in the world.

Mona Lisa with a Pizza
by Leonardo da Pepperoni

1. **What fraction of fishes is plain?** _____

2. **What fraction is striped?** _____

3. **What fraction has open mouths?** _____

4. **What fraction has their mouths closed?** _____

5. **What fraction of the pizza has only cheese?** _____

6. **What fraction of the pizza has pepperoni?** _____

7. **Five slices represent what fraction of the pizza?** _____

8. **Eight slices represent what fraction of the pizza?** _____

Georgia O'Fourth:

In the desert where I live, one often comes across a scene like this. The sky is bright. The cow is lonely. The fence is angry. How can you tell? It is picketing.

The Sky, a Cow, a Fence
by Georgia O'Fourth

9. What fraction of the cow's legs is colored? _____

10. What fraction of the cow's legs is white? _____

11. What fraction of the fence is colored? _____

12. What fraction of the fence is white? _____

Salvadore Golly:

Little Men Holding Umbrellas Falling Out of the Sky
by Salvadore Golly

This painting was inspired by a real experience I had. It started raining hard. First it rained cats and dogs. Then it rained shoes and socks. Finally, it rained little men. Some of them were wearing hats, and some were holding umbrellas.

13. What fraction of the little men are holding umbrellas? _____

14. What fraction of the men are not holding umbrellas? _____

15. What fraction of the little men are wearing hats? _____

16. What fraction of the men are not wearing hats? _____

Diane Rhombus:

This is a picture of a girl with a bad haircut making lemonade. I call it *Girl With a Bad Haircut Making Lemonade*. I tasted some of the lemonade after I finished the picture. It was delicious. P.S. The girl better get a new haircut.

Girl With a Bad Haircut Making Lemonade by Diane Rhombus

17. What fraction of the pitcher is full? _____

18. What fraction of the pitcher is empty? _____

19. What fraction of the glass is full? _____

20. What fraction of the glass is empty? _____

MORE: Draw your own artwork. When you're done, label all the fractions you can find on it.

12

Name _____

The History of Fractions: A Play in One Act

Written and Performed by the Students in Ms. Webster's Class

NARRATOR: No one knows for sure who discovered fractions. But experts suspect it had something to do with the invention of the cookie, back in the Stone Age.

STONE AGE MOM: Look, kids! It's one of those newfangled cookie things!

STONE AGE KID: I want it.

OTHER KID: No, I want it.

MOM: Now look what you did. You broke the cookie in two different-sized parts. Hmm—that gives me an idea. You take this part. And you take this other part. (*She gives a part to each kid.*)

BOTH KIDS: Gee, thanks.

NARRATOR: Experts believe this method of dividing cookies was used for thousands of years. But as the Iron Age dawned, kids began to squabble over the size of the cookie pieces they got.

IRON AGE KID: His piece is bigger than mine!

OTHER KID: No, hers is bigger!

IRON AGE KID: Hey, what's going on in there?

IRON AGE MOM: (*to Dad*) Let me borrow your ax. (*She cuts another cookie into two equal pieces.*)

DAD: What do you call this strange new method of peacemaking?

MOM: I call them HALVES.

BOTH KIDS: Wow.

NARRATOR: And so it was discovered that two halves of something had to be of equal size. (And so did three thirds, and four quarters, and five fifths.) Following this discovery, fractions flourished in the Ancient World. True, there were those years during the time of the Romans when fractions were very difficult to write and use.

ROMAN MOM: (*shopping at Roman store*) Let's see...I'd like a VIIIth of a pound of Roman Meal Bread.

ROMAN SHOPKEEPER: Oy. There must be a better way.

NARRATOR: Let's fast-forward to a More Recent Age. Two inventors, Francine Numerator and Larry Denominator, get together for an historic agreement...

FRANCINE NUMERATOR: So it's a deal. We'll call the top part of the fraction the numerator—

LARRY DENOMINATOR: —and the bottom part the denominator. Let's shake on it!

NARRATOR: And so modern fractions with numerators on the top and denominators on the bottom were born. People from all different walks of life found uses for fractions. For example, this piemaker...

PIEMAKER: My customer wants $\frac{1}{2}$ of this big pie, and $\frac{2}{3}$ of this small pie.

NARRATOR: ...this carpenter...

CARPENTER: I need to paint $\frac{3}{4}$ of this long board and $\frac{1}{4}$ of this short board.

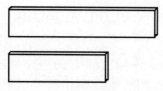

NARRATOR: ...this shepherd girl...

SHEPHERD GIRL: I need to round up $\frac{5}{6}$ of my flock.

NARRATOR: ...even this miser...

MISER: I need to save $\frac{4}{9}$ of these coins.

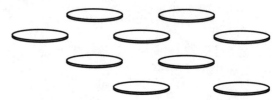

NARRATOR: Yes, fractions were extremely useful. But the most useful purpose of all wasn't discovered until the very recent past. Here we join a teacher sitting up late at night.

MS. WEBSTER: I need something that my students will find truly fun and fascinating. Wait! I've got it! Fractions!

NARRATOR: And so the best use of fractions was found: to make the students in Ms. Webster's class happy!

KID IN CLASS: Please, Ms. Webster, give us more fractions for homework...

ANOTHER KID: Oh, yes. Please! Please!

MS. WEBSTER: Well, okay. If you insist.

ALL THE KIDS: Hurray!

NARRATOR: So what are you waiting for, kids? Settle down and do these fractions!

KID: They're so cute and cuddly...

ANOTHER KID: and good for you, too!

WHOLE CLASS: Goodnight, everyone.

THE END (curtain)

PROBLEMS

1. Mark and color in $\frac{1}{2}$ of the piemaker's large pie.

2. Mark and color in $\frac{2}{3}$ of his small pie.

3. Mark and color in $\frac{3}{4}$ of the carpenter's long board.

4. Mark and color in $\frac{1}{4}$ of her short board.

5. How many sheep does the shepherd girl need to round up? _____

6. How many coins does the miser need to save? _____

7. Use any kind of drawing you like to show the fraction $\frac{3}{5}$.

8. Use any kind of drawing you like to show the fraction $\frac{7}{10}$.

9. Draw 6 shapes. Color in $\frac{1}{2}$ of the shapes.

10. Draw 12 shapes. Color in $\frac{2}{3}$ of the shapes.

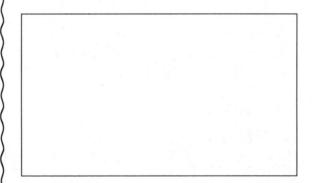

Note: *Ideas expressed in this play are solely those of Ms. Webster's class. Any resemblance to anything real is strictly a coincidence. Any historical facts that turn out to be true are likewise a coincidence. We MADE ALL THIS UP! Yours truly, Ms. Webster's Class.*

Name

Dear Ms. Fraction

1.

Dear Ms. Fraction,

There's this really cute boy in school. I'll call him Randy. He offered me $\frac{2}{3}$ of his candy bar.

Then there's this other really cute boy, Sandy. He offered me $\frac{2}{5}$ of his candy bar.

So now I don't know. Who do you think really likes me more, Randy or Sandy?

> Signed,
> CLUELESS IN SEATTLE

Dear Clueless,

I don't know who likes you more, but I can tell you who is willing to give you more candy. Look at these two candy bars.

Color in $\frac{2}{3}$ of the top one and $\frac{2}{5}$ of the bottom one. Which fraction of candy bar is bigger?

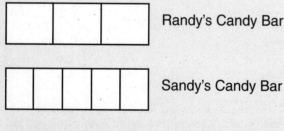

Randy's Candy Bar

Sandy's Candy Bar

> *Yours Truly,*
> *MS. FRACTION*

2.

Dear Ms. Fraction,

This girl in my class, Jennifer, really thinks I'm cool. At least she thought I was cool. Then she offered to split a Mango Fango fruit drink with me. Well, Ms. Fraction, I forgot what I was doing and drank $\frac{5}{6}$ of the Mango Fango. That made Jennifer mad. She says I'm worse than her last boyfriend, Lloyd, who drank $\frac{7}{8}$ of a Choco-Rocko shake they were sharing.

So who's worse, Lloyd or me?

> Signed,
> The Kansas City GULPer

Dear KCG,

Why don't you line up a Mango Fango next to a Choco-Rocko? **Color in $\frac{5}{6}$ of the Mango Fango and $\frac{7}{8}$ of the Choco-Rocko.** *That should tell you who's the bigger chugger.*

> *Yours Truly,*
> *MS. FRACTION*

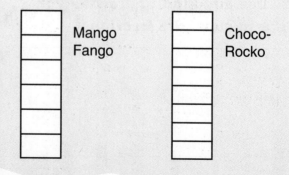

Mango Fango

Choco-Rocko

3.

Dear Ms. Fraction,

Help! I'm totally uncool. The way I see it, a cool baseball cap would make me $\frac{1}{4}$ cooler than I am now. But a totally cool haircut would make me $\frac{3}{8}$ cooler.

So which should I get, the hat or the hair?

Signed,
Uncool in UPPER ONTARIO

———————————

Dear Uncool,

Personally, I think ice cubes in your shoes would keep you the coolest. But what do I know? **To compare the two cooling methods, divide these bars and see which fraction is bigger.**

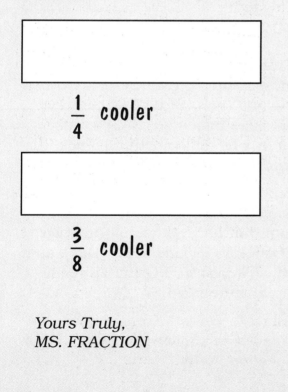

$\frac{1}{4}$ cooler

$\frac{3}{8}$ cooler

Yours Truly,
MS. FRACTION

4.

Dear Ms. Fraction,

I took a survey in school to find out what girls really like in a guy. I found that $\frac{2}{3}$ of the girls liked a guy's smile, $\frac{3}{4}$ thought a sense of humor was important, $\frac{7}{8}$ liked hair best, and $\frac{1}{7}$ felt that expensive shoes were the only thing that mattered. How can I make sense of these results?

Signed,
Survey Sam

———————————

Dear Sam,

Draw the fractions below on candy bars, pies, or whatever you like. Then list them in order from greatest to smallest. *And if you want my opinion, it's no contest: It's the shoes.*

Yours Truly,
MS. FRACTION

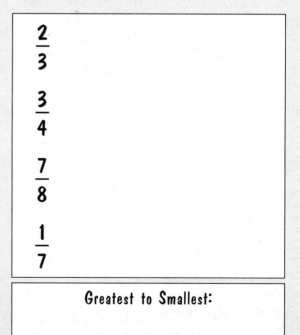

$\frac{2}{3}$

$\frac{3}{4}$

$\frac{7}{8}$

$\frac{1}{7}$

Greatest to Smallest:

____ ____ ____ ____

Name _____

Louie Lewis
Fractional Private Eye

My name is Louis Lewis. I'm a Fractional Detective. I solve fraction cases.

You know the type: fourths, eighths, sixteenths, and so on. That's why they call me Louie Lewis, FPE, Fractional Private Eye. Here's my card:

LOUIE LEWIS
Fractional Private Eye

Being an FPE is tough work, if you can get it. The hours are long. The pay is lousy. And the cases are baffling.

Take this case I had just the other day...

The Case of the Krispy Krackers

I got a call from Victor Kronsky. He's the millionaire owner of the Kronsky Krispy Krackers Kompany. You know the ones. They come in all different sizes like: WHOLES, HALVES, and FOURTHS.

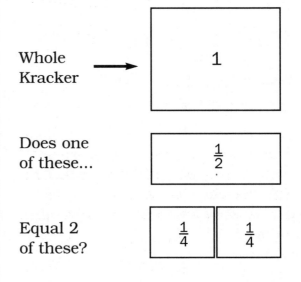

Whole Kracker → 1

Does one of these... $\frac{1}{2}$

Equal 2 of these? $\frac{1}{4}$ | $\frac{1}{4}$

Kronsky was frantic. His factory had messed up a gigantic cracker order, making thousands of FOURTHS crackers instead of HALF crackers. Unless he did something quick, his whole cracker empire was doomed!

But there was one glimmer of hope. Kronsky's cracker experts had told him that he could substitute two FOURTHS for one HALF. But was it true? Were two FOURTHS really equal to one HALF?

"Blast it, Lewis!" Kronsky roared. "I've got to know the answer to this question, NOW!!"

"Sure thing, Mr. Kronsky," I replied. "I'll get right on it."

So I got right on it. But I'm not going to tell you the answer.

Instead, on another sheet of paper, use diagrams, cutouts, or numbers to prove the following:

1. $\frac{1}{2}$ **is the same as** $\frac{2}{4}$

2. $\frac{1}{2}$ **is the same as** $\frac{4}{8}$

3. **Explain how you know your answers are true.**

Well, wouldn't you know it. No sooner had I finished that problem when Kronsky came up with a new one. And this was a doozy. He wanted me to find FOUR NEW FRACTIONS that were equal to $\frac{1}{2}$.

Can you think of 4 more fractions that are equal to $\frac{1}{2}$? Write them here.

4.    5. _____

6. _____   7. _____

Needless to say, I cracked the case.

"Lewis," Kronsky said, "you're a genius. Now think of FOUR DIFFERENT FRACTIONS that are equal to $\frac{1}{3}$."

"What for?" I asked.

"I'm coming out with a new line of crackers that are divided into

THIRDS," Kronsky said.

Write 4 fractions that are equal to $\frac{1}{3}$.

8. _____   9. _____

10. _____   11. _____

Kronsky was delighted when I finished. "Remind me to give you a bonus," he said.

"A bonus?" I said. "You haven't even paid me to begin with."

But that didn't matter. Kronsky had more problems for me. He wanted me to think of 2 fractions that were equal to $\frac{2}{3}$, $\frac{3}{4}$, $\frac{2}{5}$, and $\frac{1}{6}$. Oh well. Another day, another fraction.

Think of 2 different fractions that are equal to each fraction below. Draw a picture of each fraction if you need to.

12. $\frac{2}{3}$ = _____ _____

13. $\frac{3}{4}$ = _____ _____

14. $\frac{2}{5}$ = _____ _____

15. $\frac{1}{6}$ = _____ _____

Name _____

Martha and Steve: Simplest Form

Hello. I'm Martha Crunch, your personal fraction trainer. And this is Steve.

Say, you know what really makes me mad? Trying to do sit-ups while wearing these solid lead earrings! Every time I sit up I get bonked in the head! Boy, that makes me mad!

You know what else makes me mad? Fractions that aren't in simplest form. Look at these fractions:

$$\frac{2}{4} \qquad \frac{3}{12} \qquad \frac{14}{21}$$

They're not in simplest form. We don't like 'em like that. Do we, Steve?

RA-A-AH! EE-E-URK! NO WAY! HOW DO YOU KNOW IF A FRACTION IS WRITTEN IN SIMPLEST FORM?

Take a look at $\frac{1}{2}$ and $\frac{2}{4}$.

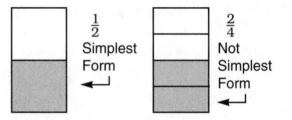

$\frac{1}{2}$ Simplest Form ←

$\frac{2}{4}$ Not Simplest Form ←

The fractions are equal. But $\frac{1}{2}$ is written in simplest form. $\frac{2}{4}$ isn't. How can you tell when a fraction is in simplest form? The easiest way is to just try reducing. If you can't reduce, the fraction is probably in simplest form.

RA-A EE-URK. BUT HOW DO YOU WRITE A FRACTION IN SIMPLEST FORM, MARTHA? WHAT ABOUT A FRACTION LIKE $\frac{14}{21}$?

No sweat, Steve! Here's one way:

Just think: what is the LARGEST number that divides evenly into both 14 and 21? That's right. It's 7.

$$\frac{14}{21} \div \frac{7}{7} = \frac{2}{3}$$

So just divide both 14 and 21 by 7. In simplest form, $\frac{14}{21}$ equals $\frac{2}{3}$.

So you see, if you do it the MARTHA CRUNCH WAY, writing fractions in simplest form can be... JUST PEACHY!

To see for yourself, try these problems. We did the first one for you.

1. $\frac{5}{10}$ = $\frac{1}{2}$

2. $\frac{6}{14}$ = _____

3. $\frac{4}{20}$ = _____

4. $\frac{20}{70}$ = _____

5. $\frac{15}{25}$ = _____

6. $\frac{12}{28}$ = _____

7. $\frac{8}{32}$ = _____

8. $\frac{18}{45}$ = _____

9. $\frac{15}{18}$ = _____

10. $\frac{24}{30}$ = _____

11. $\frac{40}{80}$ = _____

12. $\frac{36}{42}$ = _____

13. $\frac{36}{45}$ = _____

14. $\frac{28}{49}$ = _____

15. $\frac{26}{39}$ = _____

16. $\frac{48}{54}$ = _____

17. $\frac{33}{44}$ = _____

18. $\frac{40}{100}$ = _____

19. $\frac{81}{90}$ = _____

20. $\frac{64}{96}$ = _____

Hey, what'd I tell you? Was that a piece of cake or was that a piece of cake? Bye bye everyone! See you next time.

BONUS

MARTHA'S E-Z FRACTION TIPS

Hey, kids! Here's a way to make writing fractions in simplest form easier than doing 25 one-handed push-ups with your eyes closed.

First, simplify as best you can.

$$\frac{36 \div 6}{48 \div 6} = \frac{6}{8}$$

When you're done, see if you can simplify again. Sometimes you can.

$$\frac{6 \div 2}{8 \div 2} = \frac{3}{4}$$

So remember: When you're done simplifying, look again. Sometimes you can simplify one more time.

Martha Crunch's wardrobe furnished by Fraction Gal Fashions.

Name _____

Joe Trella, Fraction Fella

JOE: Welcome back, everyone. You're listening to 99 $\frac{1}{2}$ WFRA, the home of Talk Fraction Radio. I'm Joe Trella, the Fraction Fella. OK, let's go to the phones. Betty, you're on Line 2.

BETTY: Hi Joe. Love your show. I listen to it *half* the time.

JOE: Half the time? Why only half?

BETTY: Sorry, Joe. I was just joking, see. "Half" is a fraction. Get it?

JOE: I get it, Betty. What's your problem?

BETTY: It's my 14-year old daughter, Dora Mae. Whenever I give her a mixed number, like 2 $\frac{2}{3}$, she turns it into an improper fraction. You know the type. Where the top number is bigger than the bottom. Like $\frac{8}{3}$. She thinks it's funny.

JOE: Hey, I used to do the same thing when I was a kid.

BETTY: You did?

JOE: Sure. You know what you ought to do? Use reverse psychology. Give Dora Mae some improper fractions, and make her think you want her to keep 'em that way. I bet she'll turn 'em right into mixed numbers.

BETTY: Great idea, Joe. Hey, thanks a lot.

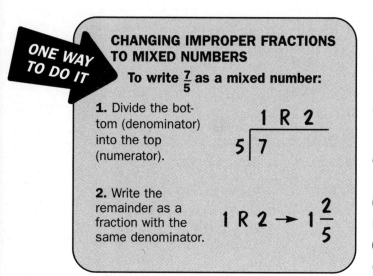

ONE WAY TO DO IT

CHANGING IMPROPER FRACTIONS TO MIXED NUMBERS

To write $\frac{7}{5}$ as a mixed number:

1. Divide the bottom (denominator) into the top (numerator).

$$5\overline{)7} \quad 1\ R\ 2$$

2. Write the remainder as a fraction with the same denominator.

$$1\ R\ 2 \rightarrow 1\frac{2}{5}$$

Write these improper fractions as mixed numbers.

1. $\frac{3}{2}$ = _____

2. $\frac{5}{3}$ = _____

3. $\frac{7}{4}$ = _____

4. $\frac{9}{2}$ = _____

5. $\frac{14}{5}$ = _____

6. $\frac{16}{5}$ = _____

7. $\frac{25}{8}$ = _____

8. $\frac{35}{6}$ = _____

9. $\frac{57}{10}$ = _____

10. $\frac{91}{15}$ = _____

JOE: Let's go to Al on Line 4. Hello, Big Al.

AL: Hello, Joe. Love your show. So anyway, what's the deal with improper fractions?

JOE: What do you mean?

AL: When I change an improper fraction to a mixed number—sometimes I find it's not in simplest form. Is this normal?

JOE: Relax, big guy. You know what my Uncle Roy used to say to me? If you need to change to sim-plest form, then go ahead and change to simplest form.

AL: Is that all there is to it, Joe?

JOE: You bet. Here's what you should do. Try writing these improper fractions as mixed numbers. Then, if they're not in simplest form, change 'em to simplest form. You'll feel much better. I promise ya.

AL: Hey, thanks Joe. These improper fractions look great. They really do. I'm gonna try 'em as soon as I hang up.

Write these improper fractions as mixed numbers. Make sure they're in simplest form.

11. $\frac{8}{6}$ = _____

12. $\frac{12}{8}$ = _____

13. $\frac{12}{3}$ = _____

14. $\frac{21}{9}$ = _____

15. $\frac{30}{12}$ = _____

16. $\frac{13}{7}$ = _____

17. $\frac{45}{36}$ = _____

18. $\frac{60}{48}$ = _____

19. $\frac{100}{24}$ = _____

20. $\frac{88}{16}$ = _____

JOE: Let's go to Pauline on Line 5.

PAULINE: Hi, Joe. It's my little brother, Danny. He's 10. Every time he sees an improper fraction, it's like he NEEDS to turn it into a mixed number.

JOE: Relax, Pauline. I think I know someone your little brother would like to meet. Her name is Dora Mae.

PAULINE: Oh, wow, Joe. That's sounds great.

JOE: So this is what you do. Have your brother turn these mixed numbers into improper fractions. And I'll see about getting him together with Dora Mae.

PAULINE: Thanks, Joe. I think my little brother's really going to like these fractions.

JOE: Not as much as he's gonna like Dora Mae.

PAULINE: You're probably right, Joe.

JOE: When it comes to fractions, Pauline, I'm always right! Anyway, that's about all we have time for. Goodnight, everyone!

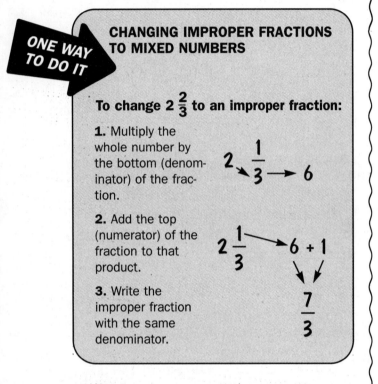

ONE WAY TO DO IT

CHANGING IMPROPER FRACTIONS TO MIXED NUMBERS

To change $2\frac{2}{3}$ to an improper fraction:

1. Multiply the whole number by the bottom (denominator) of the fraction.

$$2 \times \frac{1}{3} \rightarrow 6$$

2. Add the top (numerator) of the fraction to that product.

$$2\frac{1}{3} \rightarrow 6 + 1$$

3. Write the improper fraction with the same denominator.

$$\frac{7}{3}$$

Write these mixed numbers as improper fractions.

21. $1\frac{1}{2}$ = _____   26. $4\frac{5}{6}$ = _____

22. $2\frac{2}{3}$ = _____   27. $10\frac{1}{3}$ = _____

23. $3\frac{2}{5}$ = _____   28. $8\frac{3}{7}$ = _____

24. $4\frac{1}{2}$ = _____   29. $12\frac{1}{6}$ = _____

25. $2\frac{5}{8}$ = _____   30. $40\frac{2}{3}$ = _____

Name _____

Never More, Baltimore!

Once upon a midnight's gloom
Sat young Lenore inside her room
Doing fractions late at night,
Her heart a-pounding, full of fright.

Whereupon she heard a moaning
Then a ghastly gruesome groaning
Followed by a ghostly roar,
'Twas her pet parrot—Baltimore.

Making dreadful, squawking sounds
To mark each error that he found.
"Squawk!" he screeched. "Another blunder."
Outside was heard a crack of thunder.

"Stop!" she cried, "And don't come near.
Your squawking fills me full of fear.
Does my homework have mistakes?
Oh woe I am, my body quakes."

The bird it squawked, and then it spoke:
"Oh good Lenore, I do not joke.
Your fractions, like a wilted flower,
Start out quite sweet but end up sour.

"Like a melancholy song
They start out right but end up wrong.
Your fractions would be truly best
If in simplest form they were expressed."

"In simplest form?" said young Lenore.
"Oh please, I beg you, Baltimore.
Can you show me how it's done?
We'll work together; 'twill be fun!"

And so the bird showed young Lenore
How to reduce for Ever More.
And as she worked all through the night,
She changed her answers to make them right.

And as the morning sun shone through
She had but one group left to do.
You see it on the page below,
So do it now, and off you go.

Here are Lenore's answers. If an answer is written in simplest form, write "OK" in the blank next to the answer. If the answer is not in simplest form, write it that way.

1. $\frac{12}{16}$ = _____   9. $\frac{32}{48}$ = _____

2. $8\frac{8}{12}$ = _____   10. $\frac{48}{56}$ = _____

3. $5\frac{7}{8}$ = _____   11. $\frac{15}{80}$ = _____

4. $\frac{25}{30}$ = _____   12. $12\frac{42}{48}$ = _____

5. $14\frac{30}{40}$ = _____   13. $5\frac{12}{60}$ = _____

6. $\frac{21}{35}$ = _____   14. $\frac{16}{27}$ = _____

7. $\frac{18}{25}$ = _____   15. $7\frac{54}{81}$ = _____

8. $\frac{22}{55}$ = _____   16. $\frac{96}{144}$ = _____

Name _____

Ultra-Workout 1

Hi. Martha Crunch, your personal fractions trainer, here. And this is Ultra Workout 1!

> CAUTION: Those who complete Ultra-Workout 1 may experience moments of severe light-headedness and deep mathematical understanding.

For your own safety, DO NOT attempt Ultra-Workout 1 if any of the following is true:

- Your hair is currently on fire.

- You have a chip on your shoulder more than 17 inches long.

- You are being chased by a swarm of angry bees.

- Each of your feet weighs more than 250 pounds.

1. What fraction does this picture represent?

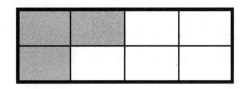

_____

2. Draw a picture that shows the fraction $\frac{7}{9}$.

_____

3. Order these fractions from smallest to largest: $\frac{3}{5}, \frac{7}{10}, \frac{1}{3}, \frac{7}{8}, \frac{1}{2}$.

_____

4. Write two fractions that are equivalent to $\frac{2}{5}$.

_____

5. Write $\frac{24}{32}$ in simplest form.

_____

6. Write $\frac{7}{4}$ as a mixed number.

_____

7. Write $4\frac{2}{3}$ as an improper fraction.

_____

Hey, wasn't that easy?
See you next time, everyone!

Name _____

Rex Roper's Believe It or Not!

Hi, kids. I'm Rex Roper, ace reporter for America's number one tabloid, the *National Gasbag Chatterer*. I'd like to tell you about some things that are so STRANGE, so BIZARRE, so downright SHOCKING that you may not believe they actually happened.

Are these things true? Well, you be the judge.

Ketchup Saves Boy's Life!

Fargo, N.D. Ten-year-old Tommy Farkus mistakenly ate liver for dinner last night.

Emergency teams rushed to the scene.

Tommy was treated for $\frac{6}{7}$ hour in the ICFU (Incredibly Crummy Food Unit) at Fargo General Hospital. After another $\frac{3}{7}$ hour of observation, he was released.

"I thought I was eating fish sticks," Tommy explained.

Doctors estimate that the boy swallowed three bites of liver weighing $\frac{3}{5}$ ounce, $\frac{2}{5}$ ounce, and $\frac{4}{5}$ ounce.

"Ketchup saved him," said Dr. Janet Janetski. "He had so much ketchup on it, he couldn't even taste the liver."

"Hey," said Tommy. "I put ketchup on everything." Write all fractions in simplest form.

1. How much time did Tommy spend in the hospital? _____

2. How much more time was spent treating Tommy than observing him? _____

3. How many ounces of liver did Tommy eat in all? _____

4. How many ounces of liver did Tommy eat in his first 2 bites? _____

5. How much liver did Tommy eat in his last 2 bites? _____

6. How much more liver did Tommy eat in his third bite than his second bite? _____

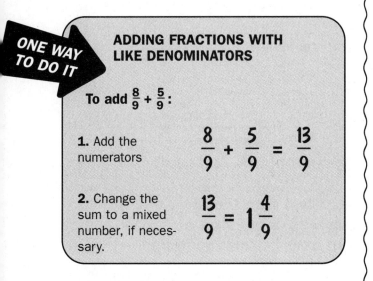

ONE WAY TO DO IT

ADDING FRACTIONS WITH LIKE DENOMINATORS

To add $\frac{8}{9} + \frac{5}{9}$:

1. Add the numerators

$$\frac{8}{9} + \frac{5}{9} = \frac{13}{9}$$

2. Change the sum to a mixed number, if necessary.

$$\frac{13}{9} = 1\frac{4}{9}$$

What to Do If YOU Are Exposed

Awful foods like liver can turn up on your plate at any time. How can you protect yourself? Here's what the experts say.

○ Don't panic. $\frac{3}{16}$ of all victims panic, but it doesn't help.

○ $\frac{1}{16}$ of victims groan. That doesn't work either.

○ $\frac{5}{16}$ of victims yowl. Don't bother.

○ $\frac{7}{16}$ of victims cover their food with ketchup. This works best.

7. What fraction of victims either panics or groans? _____

8. What fraction of victims yowls or covers the stuff with ketchup? _____

9. What fraction of victims panics, yowls, or covers with ketchup? _____

10. What fraction panics, groans, yowls, or covers with ketchup? _____

Dog Eats Homework (Really!)

Bobville, SC: Mike, a mutt owned by 12-year-old Brenda Sykes, became the first dog in history to actually eat a homework assignment.

Brenda had been making a scale model of Washington D.C. out of foot-long frankfurters when the hungry pup struck.

"He ate the whole thing," Brenda said.

Among the monuments destroyed were a $\frac{1}{12}$-pound frankfurter White House, a $\frac{5}{12}$-pound frankfurter Pentagon, a $\frac{7}{12}$-pound frankfurter Capitol, and an $\frac{11}{12}$-pound frankfurter Smithsonian.

(See questions on the next page) ➜

11. What is the total weight of the frankfurter White House and the frankfurter Pentagon? _____

12. How much more does the Smithsonian weigh than the Capitol? _____

13. How much more does the Capitol weigh than the White House? _____

14. What is the total weight of all the buildings? _____

Where Does Homework Go?

Each year, over 2 million school kids claim, "The dog ate my homework."

"But it's almost never true," said homework expert Larry Twitch.

What actually does happen to all that homework? Twitch has prepared a graph that explains the mystery.

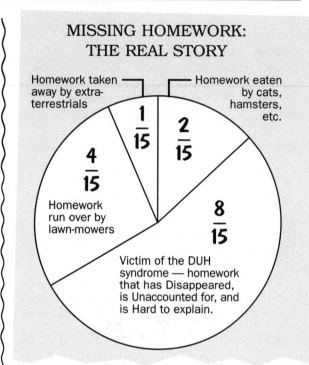

MISSING HOMEWORK:
THE REAL STORY

Homework taken away by extra-terrestrials — $\frac{1}{15}$

Homework eaten by cats, hamsters, etc. — $\frac{2}{15}$

Homework run over by lawn-mowers — $\frac{4}{15}$

Victim of the DUH syndrome — homework that has Disappeared, is Unaccounted for, and is Hard to explain. — $\frac{8}{15}$

15. What fraction of homework is eaten or run over by lawn mowers? _____

16. What fraction is run over or taken by extraterrestrials? _____

17. What fraction is eaten or becomes a victim of DUH? _____

18. What fraction is eaten, run over, or taken away by extraterrestrials? _____

Name _____

Texarkana Bernstein:
The World's Greatest Adventurer and Her Trusty Dog, Woovis

EPISODE 1: *In which Tex and Woovis meet up with the famous Johnny Hat-Size*

Howdy, and welcome to *The Tales of Texarkana Bernstein: World's Greatest Adventurer.* I'm Woovis the dog, Tex's faithful sidekick. Today's tale tells the story of one of our greatest adventures. It all started when Tex and me were doin' some explorin' down near Dodge City. We saw our old pals, Pete Forker and Jane Spoon, being carting off to jail!

"I'd have known those two horse thieves anywheres," said the sheriff. He pointed to a WANTED poster:

WANTED
Horse Rustlers

The hat sizes of these 2 desperadoes adds up to exactly 30 inches

"I measured their hats myself, and what do you know," said the Sheriff, "30 inches exactly."

"We're being framed!" Forker cried. "These aren't our hats! Our hats both measure $14\frac{5}{8}$ inches."

"Please, Tex," said Spoon. "You've got to find Johnny Hat-Size and bring him here!"

Before I go on with the story, try these problems. Use the information in the examples on the next page if you need help.

1. Suppose Forker and Spoon really do wear $14\frac{5}{8}$-inch hats. What is the sum of their hat sizes? _____

2. What is the difference between the sum of Forker's and Spoon's hat sizes and 30 inches? _____

3. Suppose Forker wears size 14 $\frac{5}{8}$. What size would Spoon need to wear to make a total of 30 inches? _____

4. Write two other mixed numbers that both add up to 30. _____

ONE WAY TO DO IT

ADDING MIXED NUMBERS WITH LIKE DENOMINATORS

Add $3\frac{3}{8}$ and $3\frac{7}{8}$:

1. Add the whole numbers and fractions separately.

$$3\frac{3}{8}$$
$$+\ 3\frac{7}{8}$$
$$\overline{\quad 6\frac{10}{8}}$$

2. Write the improper fraction in the sum as a mixed number. Then add it to the whole number.

$$6\frac{10}{8} = 6 + 1\frac{2}{8}$$

$$6$$
$$+\ 1\frac{2}{8}$$
$$\overline{\quad 7\frac{2}{8}} = 7\frac{1}{4}$$

ONE WAY TO DO IT

SUBTRACTING A MIXED NUMBER FROM A WHOLE NUMBER

Subtract $3\frac{1}{4}$ from 6:

1. It's hard to subtract a mixed number from a whole number. So write 6 as $5\frac{4}{4}$ (because $5 + \frac{4}{4} = 6$).

$$6$$
$$-\ 3\frac{1}{4}$$

2. Subtract the fractions and whole numbers separately.

$$5\frac{4}{4}$$
$$-\ 3\frac{1}{4}$$
$$\overline{\quad 2\frac{3}{4}}$$

We found Johnny near Cowtown, Texas. Sure enough, he was measurin' hat sizes. Had the whole town lined up.

"Johnny!" Tex cried. "You got to come with us. It's Spoon and Forker. They're in jail."

"Not again!" Johnny cried.

Johnny rode back to Dodge City with us. On the way, he asked if he could measured our hat sizes.

"Again?" Tex said. "You've measured my hat dozens of times before. And Woovis here's a dog. He doesn't wear hats."

So off we went, lookin' for Johnny Hat-Size. Johnny's pretty much like Johnny Appleseed, who roamed the west plantin' apple trees. Only instead of plantin' apple trees, Johnny Hat-Size measures people's hat sizes.

Old Johnny didn't care. He measured Tex at $13\frac{5}{8}$ inches and me, Woovis, at $6\frac{7}{8}$ inches.

Time for some more problems. Use the example box if you get stuck.

5. What is the sum of Tex and Woovis's hat-sizes? _____

6. How much larger is Tex's hat size than Woovis's hat size? _____

7. How much less than 30 inches is the sum of Tex's and Woovis's hat sizes? _____

8. Could Tex and Woovis be the rustlers? Why or why not? _____

_____

_____

We got back to Dodge City to find old Forker and Spoon stuck in their jail cell.

"Measure us!" they cried to Johnny.

"Can't," said the Sheriff.

"Why not?" asked Tex.

The Sheriff pointed to a sign on the wall.

ABSOLUTELY NO HAT-SIZE MEASURING OF PRISONERS!

SUBTRACTING A MIXED NUMBER FROM A MIXED NUMBER

ONE WAY TO DO IT

Subtract $4\frac{2}{3}$ from $7\frac{1}{3}$:

1. It's hard to subtract $\frac{2}{3}$ from $\frac{1}{3}$. So write $7\frac{1}{3}$ as $6\frac{4}{3}$ (because $6+\frac{4}{3}=7\frac{1}{3}$).

$$7\frac{1}{3}$$
$$-\,4\frac{2}{3}$$

2. Subtract the fraction and whole numbers separately.

$$6\frac{4}{3}$$
$$-\,4\frac{2}{3}$$
$$2\frac{2}{3}$$

"Hmm," said Tex suspiciously.

Then we caught a lucky break. Some runaway stolen horses came steamin' into town, draggin' one of the real crooks. His name was Stinky Weeden.

"Where's yer partner?" Tex asked.

"I ain't tellin'," Stinky said.

But it didn't matter, because Johnny came rushin' over. He measured old Stinky's hat size at exactly $13\frac{3}{8}$ inches. Now we had a way to figure out the hat size of Stinky's unknown partner.

9. Is the hat of Stinky's unknown partner larger or smaller than Stinky's hat? Explain. _____

_____

_____

_____

10. Forker and Spoon both claim they have a hat size of $14\frac{5}{8}$ inches. Could either of them be Stinky's partner? Explain. _____

_____

_____

_____

11. What's the hat size of Stinky's unknown partner? _____

Then Tex came up with a plan. "We don't know who Stinky's partner is," she explained, "but we do know his partner's hat size. All we need to do is measure every hat in town."

So Johnny started measuring. Only thing is, no one's hat seemed to be the right size. At the end of the day, Johnny figured only one person had gone unmeasured: the Sheriff.

"Sorry," said the Sheriff. He pointed to another sign on the wall.

ABSOLUTELY NO HAT-SIZE MEASURING OF SHERIFF!

Tex swung into action. First, she "accidentally" dropped a silver dollar on the floor. The Sheriff bent over to pick it up.

That was my cue. I quick ran over and lassoed his head with my tail. Then Johnny jumped in and measured the lasso.

"Sixteen and $\frac{5}{8}$ inches," he announced.

12. What is the sum of Stinky's and the Sheriff's hat sizes? _____

13. How much bigger was the Sheriff's hat than Stinky's hat? _____

14. How much bigger was the Sheriff's hat than Forker's and Spoon's hats? _____

15. Who do you think Stinky's partner is? Why? _____

_____

_____

_____

We should've known it'd all turn out okay. They locked up that Sheriff and let old Forker and Spoon out of jail. Our old buddies couldn't thank us enough. And Johnny Hat-Size? He kept on a measurin' and a measurin'. In time, folks said he measured nearly every single hat size in the West. And Tex and me, well, we just kept havin' adventures.

Name _____

Officer Meg O'Malley of the Fraction Police

Hi. Welcome to another episode of **The Fraction Police**, where each week you'll see...Real crimes. Real Fractions. Real Justice.

I'm Officer Meg O'Malley. Has this ever happened to you? A kid tries to help you with your homework, but gives you a WRONG ANSWER:

KID: Trying to add $\frac{1}{2} + \frac{1}{3}$, eh? That's easy. Want to see how to do it?

YOU: Well, I don't know.

KID: You'll see. My way is easier. $\frac{1}{2} + \frac{1}{3}$ equals $\frac{2}{5}$. You just add up the tops, then add up the bottoms.

YOU: Wow, that's a pretty neat trick.

KID: It's easy. And I've got plenty more tricks where that one came from.

You say you'd never fall for a trick like this? Wrong! Every year I see kids just like you fall into BFHs—Bad Fractional Habits. Pretty soon, they're committing FCs—Fractional Crimes.

A Fractional Crime may look okay, but it doesn't work. Take the FC mentioned above:

$$\frac{1}{2} + \frac{1}{3} \text{ does NOT equal } \frac{2}{5}.$$

To see why, just take a look at the evidence.

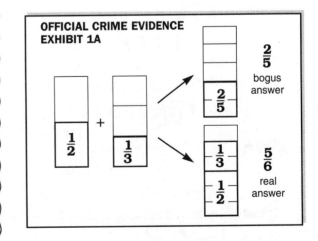

OFFICIAL CRIME EVIDENCE EXHIBIT 1A

FINDING THE LEAST COMMON DENOMINATOR

To get the correct answer, you need to find the least common denominator. How do you find the least common denominator?

Think: What's the smallest number that can be divided evenly by both 3 and 2? The answer is 6.

So 6 is the **least common denominator** for this problem.

$$\frac{1}{3} = \frac{}{6}$$

$$+ \frac{1}{2} = \frac{}{6}$$

To change both denominators to 6:

- Multiply $\frac{1}{3}$ by $\frac{2}{2}$.
- Multiply $\frac{1}{2}$ by $\frac{3}{3}$.

$$\frac{1}{3} \times \frac{2}{2} = \frac{2}{6}$$

$$+ \frac{1}{2} \times \frac{3}{3} = \frac{3}{6}$$

Now both fractions have the same denominator. When you add them, you get a sum of $\frac{5}{6}$.

$$\frac{2}{6}$$
$$+ \frac{3}{6}$$
$$\overline{\frac{5}{6}}$$

How can you avoid falling into BFHs and committing FCs? Easy. Just do these problems. Make sure your answers are in simplest form. And read my handy tips below.

1. $\dfrac{1}{4}$ (**Hint:** What's the smallest number that can be divided by both 1 and 2?)

$+ \dfrac{1}{2}$

2. $\dfrac{2}{5}$ (**Hint:** What's the smallest number that can be divided by both 5 and 10?)

$+ \dfrac{3}{10}$

3. $\dfrac{2}{3}$

$+ \dfrac{1}{6}$

4. $\dfrac{3}{5}$

$+ \dfrac{1}{3}$

5. $\dfrac{3}{8}$

$+\,\dfrac{1}{2}$

6. $\dfrac{3}{4}$

$+\,\dfrac{1}{6}$

7. $\dfrac{2}{7}$

$+\,\dfrac{5}{14}$

8. $\dfrac{1}{10}$

$+\,\dfrac{1}{2}$

9. $\dfrac{5}{8}$

$+\,\dfrac{1}{6}$

10. $\dfrac{7}{10}$

$+\,\dfrac{2}{15}$

Straight Talk from Meg O'Malley, Fraction Cop

- Be on the lookout for SFTs—Suspicious Fractional Tricks.
- Report all FCs—Fractional Crimes—to your local fractional police.
- And when you're adding fractions, for Pete's sake, USE A COMMON DENOMINATOR!

Name _____

Martha's Brain

Hello. I'm Martha Crunch, your personal fractions trainer. And this is Steve.

Welcome to my brain, everyone!

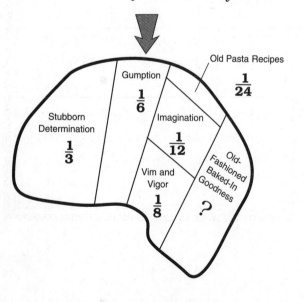

As you can see, my brain is full of good things...

...like Gumption, Vim and Vigor, and Old-Fashioned Baked-In Goodness.

These things help me with my fractions.

Plus, you'll feel better knowing that my brain has absolutely NO artificial flavorings, colorings, or preservatives.

1. What part of my brain takes up the most space? _____

_____

2. What part takes up the smallest space? _____

_____

3. Which part takes up more space—Vim and Vigor or Gumption? How much more space does it take up? _____

_____

4. Which takes up more space—Stubborn Determination or Imagination? How much more space does it take up? _____

_____

_____

_____

5. Add up all the parts of my brain except for the Old-Fashioned Baked-in Goodness. What fraction do you get? _____

6. What fraction of my brain is taken up by Old-Fashioned Baked-in Goodness? _____

7. Which two parts of my brain make up exactly 1/2 of my brain power? _____

_____

8. Which three brain parts, when added together, are equal in size to Stubborn Determination? _____

_____

9. Suppose my Old Pasta Recipes triple in size. They would now have the same size as what other brain area? _____

_____

Hey, this has been fun! For more fun with My Brain, see page 75.

And for more fun with your own brain, try my Handy Brain Tips below.

Otherwise, so long everyone! See you next time.

MARTHA'S HANDY BRAIN TIPS

TIP 1: Your brain is a muscle. Use it or lose it!

TIP 2: Math problems make your brain strong. Do 500 or more a day.

TIP 3: At night, store your brain in a cool dry place, like your head.

TIP 4: Try not to clutter your brain with too many old pasta recipes.

TIP 5: Get a complete brain tune-up every 3 months or 3,000 thoughts, whichever comes first.

Name _____

Texarkana Bernstein:
The World's Greatest Adventurer and Her Trusty Dog, Woovis

EPISODE 2: *In which Tex and Woovis get involved in another one of their rollicking adventures*

Howdy, and welcome to The Tales of Texarkana Bernstein, the World's Greatest Adventurer. I'm Woovis, Tex's trusty dog. I'm also the narrator of this story. Tex and I were out trekkin' on another one of our unforgettable journeys. Down near the Spooky-Dark Mountains we went, searchin' for fabulous fortunes, glitterin' jewels, tantalizin' treasures, and hair-raisin' adventure.

Suddenly, a piece of paper came hurtlin' through the window of our tent. It had three Secret Numbers written on it:

SN #1: $4\frac{2}{3}$

SN #2: $1\frac{1}{6}$

SN #3: $3\frac{3}{4}$

The other side had a Secret Riddle:

SECRET RIDDLE #1

Strong as an ox, light as a feather
Add the Secret Numbers together.
The answer then will become more clear
As 4 NEW Secret Numbers appear.

"Woof woof!" I said.

"Right again," Tex said. "Let's add 'em up and see what happens. We'll use that information box on the next page if we run into trouble."

1. Add Secret Numbers 1 and 2 to find Secret Number 4.
SECRET NUMBER 4 = _____

2. Add Secret Numbers 2 and 3 to find Secret Number 5.
SECRET NUMBER 5 = _____

3. Add Secret Numbers 1 and 3 to find Secret Number 6.
SECRET NUMBER 6 = _____

4. Add Secret Numbers 1, 2, and 3 to find Secret Number 7.
SECRET NUMBER 7 = _____

SECRET RIDDLE #2

The sands of Mars, the rings of Saturn
Can you see a Riddle pattern?
Strong as an ox, light as a feather
Add the NEW Secret Numbers together.

ONE WAY TO DO IT

ADDING MIXED NUMBERS WITH UNLIKE DENOMINATORS

Add $5\frac{1}{3}$ and $4\frac{7}{9}$:

1. Write the mixed numbers with a common denominator. Add the whole numbers and the fractions separately.

$$5\frac{1}{3} = 5\frac{3}{9}$$
$$+\ 4\frac{7}{9} = 4\frac{7}{9}$$
$$\overline{\qquad\quad 9\frac{10}{9}}$$

2. Write the improper fraction in the sum as a mixed number. Then add it to the whole number

$$9\frac{10}{9} = 9 + 1\frac{1}{9}$$
$$9$$
$$+\ 1\frac{1}{9}$$
$$\overline{10\frac{1}{9}}$$

Well, we did it, all right. Solved that old Riddle Number 1 as sure as my name's Woovis. Now that we'd solved Riddle 1, it was on to Riddle 2. We found it blowing among the tumbleweed.

"Listen to this," Tex said. She read the riddle aloud:

5. Add Secret Numbers 4 and 5 to find Secret Number 8.
SECRET NUMBER 8 = _____

6. Add Secret Numbers 4 and 6 to find Secret Number 9.
SECRET NUMBER 9 = _____

7. Add Secret Numbers 4 and 7 to find Secret Number 10.
SECRET NUMBER 10 = _____

8. Add Secret Numbers 5 and 6 to find Secret Number 11.
SECRET NUMBER 11 = _____

9. Add Secret Numbers 5 and 7 to find Secret Number 12.
SECRET NUMBER 12 = _____

10. Add Secret Numbers 6 and 7 to find Secret Number 13.
SECRET NUMBER 13 = _____

11. Add Secret Numbers 4, 5, 6, and 7 to find Secret Number 14.

SECRET NUMBER 14 = _____

Well, we were so busy goin' along there, addin' up the Secret Numbers that we didn't realize we'd fallen in a pit of poisonous snakes. And we surely didn't hear Tex's EVIL ARCH RIVAL, Miles Portly, sneak up on us.

"Tex," Portly snickered, "I want to thank you and your scrungy dog for leadin' me straight to the treasure."

"Treasure?!" we said. And sure enough, underneath all the snakes was a treasure chest with a combination lock. Written on the chest were these words:

Salsa, Cha-cha, do the Mambo
Here's how you get the Secret Combo:
The lock will open without a fight
If you go this many turns, right-left-right...
Right: The sum of Secret Numbers 1 and 11
Left: Now add Numbers 10 and 7
Right: Add Secret Numbers 14 and 9
And everything will turn out fine.

Old Miles Portly demanded we give him the Secret Numbers. Which we did. But Tex wasn't concerned.

"Don't worry," she said. "Old Miles will make a mistake."

Which he did. Old Miles figured that the numbers for the combination lock were 17, 25, and 44.

12. Which combination number did Miles get correct? _____

13. Which numbers did Miles get wrong? _____ _____

14. What is the correct combination? _____ _____ _____

Well, after old Miles tried out the wrong combination, a whole bunch of stuff happened: the pit caved in, the snakes got loose, et cetera, et cetera. In the end, old Miles found himself in a bucket of mud. Haw, haw.

Meanwhile, Tex and I got the treasure. But being the nice, kindly hombres we are, we decided to give it all away. We pretty much ended up with what we began with: nothin' much but a good adventure.

Name _____

Billy Doogan, Roving Weather Man

SCENE 1: *A beautiful park. A boy and a girl carry a picnic basket.*

GIRL: This is going to be a great picnic.

NARRATOR: Overhead, a big, black rain cloud blocks out the sun.

BOY: Oh, no! Our picnic will be ruined!

NARRATOR: Suddenly, a kid in a super-hero suit appears.

GIRL: Who are you?

BILLY: I'm Billy Doogan, Roving Weather Man!

BOY: Huh??

BILLY: Here's my complete forecast: Currently, it's $76\frac{1}{2}$ degrees in the park. We'll reach a high of 82 and a low of $68\frac{3}{4}$ degrees today. Normal high is $83\frac{1}{3}$ degrees. Normal low is 69 degrees. I expect $1\frac{1}{4}$ inches of rain from that big black cloud. That will give us a total of 10 inches of rain so far this month.

BOY: B-b-but how do you know all this?

BILLY: I'm Billy Doogan, Roving Weather Man! I roam around, doing what I can, helping people with their weather problems.

NARRATOR: Suddenly, Billy disappears.

BOY: Who was that guy?

GIRL: He's Billy Doogan, Roving Weather Man.

BOY: I know, but who was he really?

GIRL: Look, we can't talk now. We've got to get out of here. It's going to rain!

PROBLEMS

1. How many degrees does Billy expect the temperature to rise this afternoon? _____

2. What is the difference between today's expected high and low? _____

3. What is the difference between the current temperature and the expected low? _____

4. What is the difference between the normal high and the normal low? _____

5. Find the difference between today's expected high and the normal high. _____

6. Find the difference between today's expected low and the normal low. _____

7. How many inches of rain have fallen this month before today? _____

SCENE 2: _Man and woman in a movie theater, waiting for a movie to start._

MAN: Oh my gosh! We left the ice cream in the trunk of the car. We have to take it home or it'll melt.

WOMAN: Isn't there anything we can do?

NARRATOR: Suddenly, Billy Doogan appears!

GIRL: Who are you?

BILLY: I'm Billy Doogan, Roving Weather Man! But don't worry. The temperature is now $30\frac{3}{4}$ degrees. Your ice cream won't start to melt until the temperature reaches 32 degrees.

WOMAN: Do you mean we can stay and watch the movie?

BILLY: That's right. My forecast calls for a high of $34\frac{1}{2}$ degrees, but your movie will be long over by then.

MAN: Thank goodness. You've saved us, Roving Weather Man!

BILLY: Hey, I'm only doing my job. By the way, winds are calm at $4\frac{2}{3}$ miles per hour. They should increase to about 6 miles per hour tonight. My overnight forecast calls for $\frac{2}{3}$ of an inch of snow. This should give us a total of 5 inches on the ground. Good day, and good weather to you.

NARRATOR: Billy disappears.

MAN: What a great guy!

WOMAN: I wonder why he does what he does?

MAN: Beats me. Oh well, let's sit back and enjoy our movie.

MORE PROBLEMS

8. How many degrees will it have to warm up before the ice cream starts to melt? _____

9. How many degrees above freezing will today's high be? _____

10. What is the difference between the current temperature and today's expected high? _____

11. By how many miles per hour does Billy predict the wind speed will increase? _____

12. How many inches of snow are on the ground right now? _____

13. How many inches of snow would have to fall to have a foot of snow on the ground by tonight? _____

Name _____

Ultra-Workout, Too!

Howdy, folks. This is Woovis the dog, your host for Ultra-Workout, Too!

Now, folks often ask me, "How do you know when you've solved a problem correctly, Woovis?"

The answer is simple. Just look down at your tail. It usually wags when the answer is correct.

Of course, if you don't HAVE a tail, then maybe you better think of somethin' else. Like checkin' your answer or somethin'.

Anyway, go ahead and do these problems. And for goodness sakes—pay attention to your tail!

1. Add $\frac{4}{15} + \frac{7}{15}$. _____

2. I love Cheez-Whip. Suppose I found a $2\frac{7}{12}$ pound can of it. I would probably eat $1\frac{5}{12}$ pounds of it and save the rest. **How much would I save?** _____

3. Find the sum of $\frac{4}{9}$ **and** $\frac{1}{6}$. _____

4. Here's one of my favorite recipes. I call it Cheez-Whip Soo-Flay a là Woovis: Mix $\frac{1}{4}$ cup of flour, $\frac{3}{8}$ cup of smashed dog biscuits, and $\frac{1}{3}$ cup of Cheez-Whip. **How many cups does this recipe make?** _____

5. Subtract $4\frac{3}{10}$ **from** $7\frac{3}{5}$. _____

6. I can smell Nacho-Flavored Cheez-Whip from 6 blocks away. I can smell Regular Cheez-Whip from only $4\frac{2}{3}$ blocks away. **How much closer do I need to get to smell Regular Cheez-Whip?** _____

7. Add $4\frac{7}{8}$ **to** $8\frac{7}{12}$. _____

8. Did you know you can use Cheez-Whip to power your car? Suppose you filled your gas tank with $15\frac{1}{4}$ gallons of Cheez-Whip. Then you drove around for a while and burned up $6\frac{3}{5}$ gallons. **How many gallons would be left?** _____

Name

Emily Taproot, Fractional Poet

Hello. I'm Emily Taproot, Fractional Poet. And today I'd like to share some of my favorite fractional poems with you.

What do fractions mean to me? Read this poem and find out.

The Power of Fractions

I am fraction
Hear me roar.
In the kitchen
Through the door.
Someone dropped me
On the floor.
By the way...
What's $\frac{5}{6}$ of 54?

1. Well, what is $\frac{5}{6}$ of 54? _____

If you don't know, try this example.

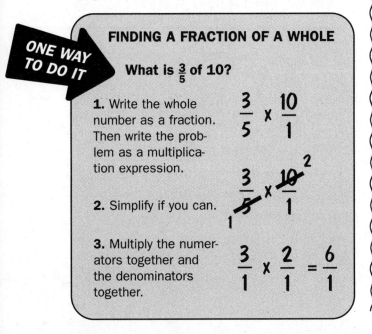

ONE WAY TO DO IT

FINDING A FRACTION OF A WHOLE

What is $\frac{3}{5}$ of 10?

1. Write the whole number as a fraction. Then write the problem as a multiplication expression.

$$\frac{3}{5} \times \frac{10}{1}$$

2. Simplify if you can.

$$\frac{3}{\cancel{5}_1} \times \frac{\cancel{10}^2}{1}$$

3. Multiply the numerators together and the denominators together.

$$\frac{3}{1} \times \frac{2}{1} = \frac{6}{1}$$

Fractions can reveal our inner feelings:

Inner Feelings

I'm sad. I'm blue.
What's $\frac{3}{4}$ of 32?
I don't know.
How about you?

2. Well, what is $\frac{3}{4}$ of 32? _____

Fractions can tell us about love...

Fragments of Love

A cloudy day.
My love and I walk by the bay.
And then, he surprises
As a fundamental question arises:
"What's $\frac{3}{10}$ of 90?" he inquires.
My heart burns with a thousand fires.

3. OK, what is $\frac{3}{10}$ of 90? _____

Fractions can tell us about our deepest hungers...

Thoughts on a Spring Day

You know what I'd like?
To solve a fraction
While riding my bike.
Now that would be fun.
Like: What's $\frac{1}{3}$ of 21?
Or: What's $\frac{3}{8}$ of 24?
Dare I do more?
Or shall I fall asleep and start to snore?

4. What is $\frac{1}{3}$ of 21 _____
and $\frac{3}{8}$ of 24? _____

...our happiest joys...

The Joy of Fractions

The satisfaction
I get from a fraction
Is something that sticks...
All the way from my feet
To the bottom of my appendix.
So tell me, please...
What's $\frac{2}{3}$ of 36?

5. So what is $\frac{2}{3}$ of 36? _____

...and our biggest frustrations.

A Cry for Help

Oh drat. Oh gee.
What's $\frac{1}{3}$ of 33?
I don't know.
Can you tell me?

6. Well, what is $\frac{1}{3}$ of 33? _____

But sometimes you just want to have fun:

Some Poems Are Just Plain Fun

Occasionally a poem is just plain fun.
But this ain't the one.
This one is a bore:
What's $\frac{7}{8}$ of 64?

7. Well, what is $\frac{7}{8}$ of 64? _____

Thank you for sharing these poems with me. Here's a little going-away gift for you.

The End

Oh wow. What fun.
8. What's $\frac{2}{3}$ of 21?
After you tell me
You'll be done. _____

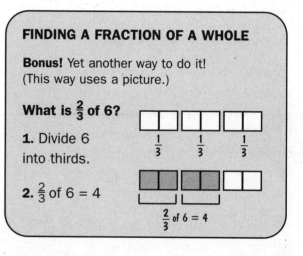

FINDING A FRACTION OF A WHOLE

Bonus! Yet another way to do it! (This way uses a picture.)

What is $\frac{2}{3}$ of 6?

1. Divide 6 into thirds.

2. $\frac{2}{3}$ of 6 = 4

$\frac{2}{3}$ of 6 = 4

Name

The Frackie Awards

FRACKIE AWARDS

JERRY: LIVE from Hollywood, welcome to the Third Annual Fractional Academy Awards. I'm your co-host, Jerry Fragment.

DEBBIE: And I'm Debbie Slash, your other co-host, reminding you that this year's Frackies are brought to you by Common Denominator: When it comes to fractions, we're the common denominator.

JERRY: Well, Debbie, without any further ado, let's get to the awards. This first Frackie goes to the Best Supporting Fraction in a Comedy, Drama, or Action Sequence.

DEBBIE: Our first nominee is Vickie Ganoosh in *Cheese Man: The Movie.*

JERRY: As you'll recall, Cheese Man is the story of a man whose entire body turns to cheese.

DEBBIE: The local townspeople think Cheese Man is evil. But all Cheese Man really wants is a hug from Vickie Ganoosh. Here she is in a powerful fractional scene:

Scene from
CHEESE MAN: THE MOVIE

VICKIE GANOOSH: Oh, Cheese Man. I DO love you. Before, I only loved $\frac{2}{3}$ of $\frac{1}{2}$ of you. Later, I loved $\frac{3}{4}$ of $\frac{2}{3}$ of you. But now, I love all of you. Or at least $\frac{4}{5}$ of $\frac{7}{8}$ of you.

CHEESE MAN: Me never so happy in whole life. Me not think so good because brain made of cheese. But if me could think, $\frac{5}{6}$ of $\frac{3}{4}$ of me would feel happy. That some powerful happiness, Vickie Ganoosh.

FINDING A FRACTION OF A FRACTION

What is $\frac{1}{2}$ of $\frac{1}{2}$?

ONE WAY TO THINK ABOUT IT

1. Start with $\frac{1}{2}$.

2. Take $\frac{1}{2}$ of that.

3. That shows you that $\frac{1}{2}$ of $\frac{1}{2}$ is $\frac{1}{4}$.

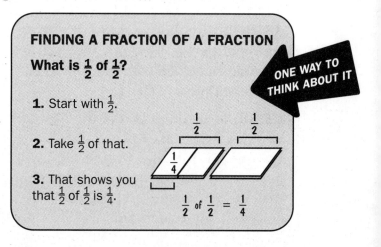

$$\frac{1}{2} \text{ of } \frac{1}{2} = \frac{1}{4}$$

(Thunderous applause from audience)

1. Before, Vickie only loved $\frac{2}{3}$ of $\frac{1}{2}$ of the Cheese Man. What is $\frac{2}{3}$ of $\frac{1}{2}$? _____

2. Later, Vickie loved $\frac{3}{4}$ of $\frac{2}{3}$ of the Cheese Man. What is $\frac{3}{4}$ of $\frac{2}{3}$? _____

3. What fraction of the Cheese Man does Vickie love now? _____

4. What fraction of the Cheese Man feels happy? _____

ONE WAY TO DO IT

MULTIPLYING A FRACTION BY A FRACTION

What is $\frac{3}{5} \times \frac{5}{6}$?

1. Simplify if you can.

$$\frac{\cancel{3}^{\,1}}{\cancel{5}_{\,1}} \times \frac{\cancel{5}^{\,1}}{\cancel{6}_{\,2}} =$$

2. Multiply the numerators together and the denominators together.

$$\frac{1}{1} \times \frac{1}{2} = \frac{1}{2}$$

JERRY: *(Sniffs away a tear.)* Wasn't that wonderful, Debbie? Our second Frackie nominee comes from the comedy *Dull as Dirt.*

DEBBIE: *Dull as Dirt* is the story of two guys who are dull as dirt. They're so dull that their dullness becomes a secret weapon for the FBI. Here's a scene where an FBI scientist interviews them:

Scene from
DULL AS DIRT

SCIENTIST: Think real hard on this one. I have $\frac{3}{4}$ of a cookie. What is $\frac{1}{2}$ of that $\frac{3}{4}$?

DULL GUY: Huh?

SCIENTIST: Try this one: I have $\frac{3}{5}$ of a pizza. What's $\frac{5}{6}$ of that?

OTHER DULL GUY: Whuh?

SCIENTIST: OK, what's $\frac{5}{8}$ of $\frac{16}{25}$ of a pie?

BOTH DULL GUYS: Huh?

(Curtain goes up. Another thunderous applause)

5. The scientist asked what $\frac{1}{2}$ of $\frac{3}{4}$ of a cookie was. What is it? _____

6. What is $\frac{3}{5}$ of $\frac{5}{6}$ of a pizza? _____

7. What is $\frac{5}{8}$ of $\frac{16}{25}$ of a pie? _____

DEBBIE: Our third nominee comes from the exciting thriller, *Murder on the Fraction Express.* Listen as bungling detective Lon Largely and his sidekick Pokey figure out who the criminal must be.

Scene from
MURDER ON THE FRACTION EXPRESS

LON LARGELY: *(Fingers his slim mustache)* Wait! Alice was in the parlor for $\frac{2}{3}$ of an hour, right? So she and Bob must have been drinking tea for $\frac{1}{2}$ of that time. Meanwhile, Carmen and Ron were on a walk that lasted $\frac{3}{4}$ of an hour. They were out of sight for $\frac{5}{6}$ of that time.

POKEY: Which means the money was left unattended for only $\frac{1}{6}$ of an hour. If Digby spent $\frac{3}{5}$ of that time playing the violin, it means that...

LON: ...Monica Monroe MUST have done it. Brilliant, Pokey. Simply brilliant.

(Curtain goes up. Another thunderous applause.)

8. What fraction of an hour did Alice and Bob spend in the parlor drinking tea? _____

9. What fraction of an hour did Carmen and Ron spend out of sight? _____

10. What fraction of an hour did Digby spend playing the violin? _____

JERRY: Wow! That was exciting. And now, the moment we've all been waiting for. Do you have the envelope, Debbie?

DEBBIE: I sure do, Jerry. Oh my gosh! You're not going to believe this, Jerry. It's a three-way tie for the Frackie!

JERRY: Unbelievable! Vickie Ganoosh, the Dull Guys, and Lon Largely all win Frackies. Come on up here, everyone!

(Thunderous applause as Vickie, the Dull Guys, and Lon walk up to the stage)

DEBBIE: Oh, no. We only have $\frac{4}{5}$ of a minute for all 4 of them to give their speeches. What should we do?

JERRY: Each person gets $\frac{1}{4}$ of that $\frac{4}{5}$ of a minute to speak.

DEBBIE: Great idea, Jerry. Good night, everyone!

11. For what fraction of a minute does each person get to speak? _____

12. For how many seconds does each person get to speak? (Hint: How many seconds are in a minute?) _____

Name

Emily Taproot's
Winky-Tinky Tigglesworth

Hello. I'm Emily Taproot, Fractional Poet. Today I'd like to talk to you about reciprocals. Here's a very small poem about reciprocals: "Reciprocal, reciprocal..."

Ugh! Nothing seems to rhyme with the word reciprocal! Fortunately, it's easier to *find* a reciprocal than to make up a poem about one.

How do you find reciprocals? Easy. Just turn the number or fraction upside down. Here are some examples.

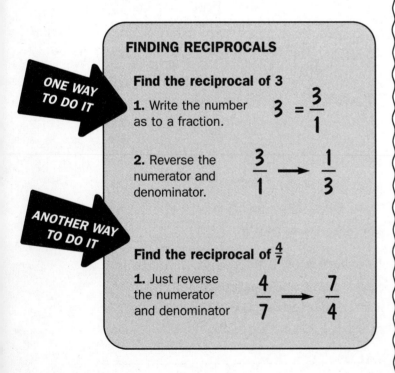

FINDING RECIPROCALS

ONE WAY TO DO IT

Find the reciprocal of 3

1. Write the number as to a fraction.

$$3 = \frac{3}{1}$$

2. Reverse the numerator and denominator.

$$\frac{3}{1} \longrightarrow \frac{1}{3}$$

ANOTHER WAY TO DO IT

Find the reciprocal of $\frac{4}{7}$

1. Just reverse the numerator and denominator

$$\frac{4}{7} \longrightarrow \frac{7}{4}$$

Hey wait. I just remembered a poem that is about reciprocals.

Winky-Tinky Tigglesworth

Winky-Tinky Tigglesworth
Found the reciprocal of 1.
"I turned it upside-down," said Winky.
"Hey, this is sort of fun."

Winky-Tinky Tigglesworth
Computed the reciprocal of 50
"That's good," Winky's mother said.
"You'll grow up fair and thrifty."

Winky-Tinky Tigglesworth
Got the reciprocal of 7 over 18
"It's neither small nor big," said Winky.
"It's kind of in-between."

Winky-Tinky Tigglesworth
Found the reciprocal of 2.
"I think I'm getting the hang of it," he said.
"Though the concept's still quite new."

Winky-Tinky Tigglesworth
Discovered the reciprocal of 3 over 8.
"It's a lot like flipping coins," he said.
"I think this is working out great."

Winky-Tinky's fish was named
"The Reciprocal of 4 over 9."
"It's kind of an awkward name," he said.
"But I think he likes it fine."

Winky-Tinky Tigglesworth
Got stuck on the reciprocal of $1\frac{2}{3}$.
"I feel so frustrated right now," Winky said.
"I'm at a loss for words."

Winky-Tinky was tired after finding
The reciprocal of 1 over 8.
"To you it might seem early," he said.
"But to me it's very, very late."

"Fshew!" said Winky-Tinky
As he found the reciprocal of $\frac{4}{33}$.
"I feel much better now," Winky said.
"Let's have a cup of tea."

Find the reciprocals of the numbers and fractions in the poem

1. Reciprocal of 1: _____

2. Reciprocal of 2: _____

3. Reciprocal of 50: _____

4. Reciprocal of $\frac{3}{8}$: _____

5. Reciprocal of $\frac{7}{18}$: _____

6. Reciprocal of $\frac{4}{9}$: _____

7. Reciprocal of $1\frac{2}{3}$: _____

8. Reciprocal of $\frac{1}{8}$: _____

9. Reciprocal of $\frac{4}{33}$: _____

Here are some bonus reciprocals to find

10. Reciprocal of $2\frac{1}{2}$: _____

11. Reciprocal of $\frac{12}{16}$ in simplest form: _____

12. Reciprocal of $\frac{50}{50}$ in simplest form: _____

Super Bonus

13. What is the reciprocal of $\frac{2}{3}$? _____

14. What is the reciprocal of your answer to problem 13? _____

15. What is the reciprocal of $\frac{5}{7}$? _____

16. What is the reciprocal of your answer to problem 15? _____

17. Make up a rule about finding the reciprocal of a reciprocal. (Hint: See your answers to problems 13 through 16.)

_____

_____

_____

Name _____

Louie Lewis: The Case of the Flipping Fractions

My name is Louis Lewis. I'm a Fractional Detective. I specialize in fractional cases. That's why they call me:

LOUIE LEWIS
Fractional Private Eye

Sometimes an FPE gets a weird case. For example, the other day this guy Mopey Mulligan calls me up. Mopey's a joker. Always trying to be funny.

"Hey Louie," he said. "Long time, ABDEFGHIJKLMNOPQRSTUVWXYZ."

"Excuse me?" I said.

"It's the alphabet without a 'C,'" he explained. "Long time, no C.' Get it? No see?"

"I get it," I said. "So what's up, Mopey?"

"I'm in a jam, Louie," he said. "Punky Pearson paid me a whole bunch of money to do these division problems."

"What's wrong with division?" I asked. "You were always good at division, Mope."

"Yeah," he said. "But this is FRAC-TIONS, Louie. Look at this sample problem that Punky did."

$$\frac{2}{3} \div \frac{4}{9} = 1\frac{1}{2}$$

"Hmm," I said. "Are you sure this answer's right?"

"Positive," he said. "You gotta help me figure this out, Louie. You just GOTTA."

Suddenly I noticed something Punky had written on the side of the page:

$$\frac{2}{3} \div \frac{4}{9} = \frac{2}{3} \times \frac{9}{4}$$

"What does it mean?" Mopey asked.

And then it hit me. Punky was using the old reciprocal trick! "Of course," I cried. "He just flipped and multiplied!"

"Flipped and multiplied?" Mopey said. "What's that? Sounds like a circus trick they do on the flying trapeze."

"Not at all," I said. "Just look at this example."

> **ONE WAY TO DO IT**
>
> ### DIVIDING FRACTIONS
>
> What is $\frac{2}{3} \div \frac{4}{9}$?
>
> **1.** Find the reciprocal of the fraction you're dividing by. Invert, or flip the numerator and denominator.
>
> $$\frac{2}{3} \div \frac{4}{9} = \frac{2}{3} \times \frac{9}{4}$$
>
> **2.** Then multiply as you would normally.
>
> $$\frac{\cancel{2}^{1}}{3} \times \frac{\cancel{9}^{3}}{\cancel{4}_{2}} = \frac{3}{2} = 1\frac{1}{2}$$

"I get it," Mopey said. "When you divide fractions you just FLIP and MULTIPLY. That's how you divide fractions."

"Flip and multiply," I said. "That's the ticket."

Mopey was all smiles. "You're the greatest, Louie!" he cried. "What do I owe you?"

But I just shook my head. I didn't need any reward. For me, just solving the case was reward enough. My job was done.

You, of course, have one more job to do. You need to solve the problems below. Once you do that we can truly say:

THIS CASE IS CLOSED.

1. $\frac{2}{3} \div \frac{4}{9} =$ $1\frac{1}{2}$ _____

2. $\frac{7}{9} \div \frac{7}{18} =$ _____

3. $\frac{5}{8} \div \frac{3}{16} =$ _____

4. $\frac{3}{5} \div \frac{6}{25} =$ _____

5. $\frac{7}{8} \div \frac{1}{12} =$ _____

6. $\frac{3}{4} \div \frac{9}{16} =$ _____

7. $\frac{5}{7} \div \frac{10}{21} =$ _____

8. $6 \div \frac{2}{3} =$ _____

9. $12 \div \frac{3}{4} =$ _____

10. $\frac{3}{10} \div \frac{18}{25} =$ _____

11. $\frac{16}{25} \div \frac{24}{35} =$ _____

12. $\frac{2}{3} \div \frac{8}{33} =$ _____

13. $\frac{15}{16} \div \frac{9}{32} =$ _____

14. $\frac{24}{49} \div \frac{6}{7} =$ _____

15. $\frac{11}{24} \div \frac{33}{40} =$ _____

Name

Officer Meg O'Malley: Episode 2

Hi. Meg O'Malley here. Welcome to another episode of The Fraction Police. See that kid? We'll call her Wendy.

Wendy was a kid who thought she knew all the answers. She was smart. She was tough. She was building a tree house. When it came time to order wood for the roof, the lumber store clerk asked, "How many square yards do you want?"

As I said, Wendy was smart. She looked at her plans.
Then she thought, "I'll multiply $2\frac{1}{4}$ by $1\frac{1}{3}$."

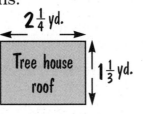

Which was correct. But here's where she made her big mistake. She multiplied the whole numbers and fractions separately.

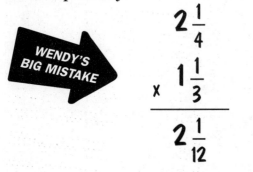

$$\begin{array}{r} 2\frac{1}{4} \\ \times\ 1\frac{1}{3} \\ \hline 2\frac{1}{12} \end{array}$$

WENDY'S BIG MISTAKE

That might sound right. But it's WRONG! It doesn't work! It's a FC—a Fractional CRIME!

You can probably guess what happened from here.

Wendy ordered the wood. The wood was the wrong size.

And guess what happened when it rained on Wendy's tree house?

WENDY GOT WET!!!

Is there a moral to our story? Don't build tree houses in rainy places, perhaps. But more importantly, don't commit FCs or fall into BFHs—Bad Fractional Habits. Learn how to multiply mixed numbers correctly.

ONE WAY TO DO IT

Multiply: $2\frac{1}{4} \times 1\frac{1}{3}$

1. Write the mixed numbers as improper fractions:

$$\frac{9}{4} \times \frac{4}{3} =$$

2. Multiply as you normally would:

$$\frac{\cancel{9}^{3}}{4} \times \frac{\cancel{4}^{1}}{\cancel{3}_{1}} = \frac{3}{1} = 3$$

Don't worry about Wendy. We straightened her out. Fixed her roof, too. When she multiplies fractions now, she does it the RIGHT WAY.

But don't be fooled. What happened to Wendy could happen to you. I've seen it a thousand times.

How can you avoid turning Wendy's UHS (Unhappy Story) into your own UHS? Simple. Just do these problems —and read my handy tips below.

Straight Talk from Meg O'Malley, Fraction Cop

- Be on the lookout for SFTs— suspicious fractional tricks.

- Report all FCs—fractional crimes— to your local fractional police.

- And for Pete's sake, always WRITE MIXED NUMBERS AS IMPROPER FRACTIONS when you multiply!

1. $1\frac{2}{3} \times 1\frac{1}{5} =$ _____

2. $1\frac{3}{4} \times 1\frac{1}{3} =$ _____

3. $3\frac{1}{3} \times 1\frac{7}{8} =$ _____

4. $1\frac{1}{6} \times 9 =$ _____

5. $2\frac{2}{9} \times 3\frac{3}{5} =$ _____

6. $2\frac{3}{4} \times \frac{4}{5} =$ _____

7. $1\frac{13}{15} \times 1\frac{4}{21} =$ _____

8. $1\frac{13}{27} \times 1\frac{1}{8} =$ _____

9. $6\frac{1}{8} \times 1\frac{11}{21} =$ _____

10. $3\frac{3}{20} \times 1\frac{23}{27} =$ _____

ONE WAY TO DO IT

Bonus Tip! This method works for DIVISION, too. Check out this example:

Divide: $1\frac{3}{7} \div 3\frac{1}{3}$

1. Write the mixed numbers as improper fractions.

$$\frac{10}{7} \div \frac{10}{3} =$$

3. Substitute the reciprocal of the number you're dividing by.

$$\frac{10}{7} \times \frac{3}{10} =$$

4. Multiply normally.

$$\frac{\cancel{10}^{1}}{7} \times \frac{3}{\cancel{10}_{1}} = \frac{3}{7}$$

Now try these problems:

11. $2\frac{2}{5} \div 1\frac{1}{5} =$ _____

12. $2\frac{1}{10} \div 14 =$ _____

Name _____

Yucky Cooking with Mr. Pierre

Welcome to Yucky Cooking. I'm Mr. Pierre. People ask me all the time, "What is Yucky Cooking, Mr. Pierre?" I tell them that Yucky Cooking is more than just cooking with yucky food. It's a whole way of putting together poor-quality ingredients so they look yucky, taste yucky, and smell yucky.

Now suppose you're having a dinner party for people you don't like so much. Do you serve them your best recipes? Of course not! You serve them Yucky Cooking.

Here's a good recipe for a not-so-special appetizer which I call Sad Sack Salad:

Sad Sack Salad

In an old sack, mix:

- $2\frac{1}{2}$ ounces wilted brown lettuce
- $1\frac{1}{8}$ ounces egg shells
- $1\frac{3}{8}$ ounces coffee grounds

Pour into a pan. Heat 2 hours until it turns to a thick mud and sticks to the pan. Chip off with a chisel or screwdriver.

1. In all, how many ounces of ingredients are in Sad Sack Salad? _____

2. Suppose you divided the Sad Sack Salad into 4 equal portions. How many ounces would each portion contain? _____

3. Suppose you put $\frac{3}{5}$ of the salad in a bowl. How many ounces of salad would be in the bowl? _____

4. How many $\frac{5}{6}$-ounce servings could you get from the recipe? _____

Here's a way to make a delicious ham not worth eating. I served this to a guest once and she ran screaming from the table. Now that's Yucky Cooking! I call this recipe Shriveled Ham Jubilee:

Shriveled Ham Jubilee

Place one good-sized ham in an old bucket. Cook for several days at a high temperature until it shrivels to a fraction of its original size. Ham is done when foul black smoke comes out of the bucket.

5. Cooking for 2 days shrinks a $3\frac{3}{4}$-pound ham to $\frac{2}{3}$ its original size. How many pounds is this? _____

6. Cooking for a week shrinks a $3\frac{3}{4}$-pound ham to $\frac{1}{10}$ its original size. How many pounds is this? _____

7. To dry out the ham faster, Mr. Pierre likes to divide the ham into $\frac{3}{4}$-pound pieces before cooking. How manypiecescan he make from a $3\frac{3}{4}$-pound ham? _____

8. Say Mr. Pierre cuts a $3\frac{3}{8}$ pound ham into $1\frac{1}{8}$-pound pieces. How many pieces will he have? _____

No bad meal is complete without a bad dessert. Here's an especially awful dessert that uses up all your unwanted leftovers. I call it Nuked Ice Cream Surprise:

Nuked Ice Cream Surprise

In a tightly-covered plastic dish, put:

- 1 ounce of ice cream (any flavor)
- $\frac{5}{6}$ ounces of leftover Sad Sack Salad
- $1\frac{1}{12}$ ounces of leftover Shriveled Ham Jubilee

Microwave until mixture explodes. Scrape off walls of microwave. Top with soggy potato chips.

9. How many total ounces of ingredients does the recipe call for? _____

10. If the dessert is divided evenly into 5 portions, how many ounces will each portion weigh? _____

11. Suppose you divided the dessert into portions that weigh $\frac{5}{12}$ ounces each. How many portions would you have? _____

12. Suppose you divided the dessert into 14 equal portions. How much would each portion weigh? _____

Name

Martha Crunch and Her Amazing Fraction Workout Video

Hi. I'm Martha Crunch, your personal fractions trainer. And this is Steve.

Listen to what folks are saying about **Martha Crunch's Amazing Fraction Workout Video.**

BEFORE

Larry G.
My imagination was dull as a butter knife.

Rosa M.
I was boring. How boring? Sometimes I even put myself to sleep.

AFTER

Larry G.
I feel great! My imagination slices and dices through ideas like a knife through cheese.

Rosa M.
Talk about AMAZING! My thoughts are 35 percent more interesting. What a difference!

Sound too good to be true?
It's NOT.

For a limited time, you too can enjoy the benefits of **Martha Crunch's Amazing Fraction Workout Video** in the comfort of your home.

RA-A-AH! EE-E-URK! WHERE DO I SIGN UP?

Right here, Steve.

For a limited time only, you can try WORKOUT #1 of the **Amazing Fraction Workout** ABSOLUTELY FREE!

If you don't absolutely love it, just return the unused fractions for a COMPLETE MONEY-BACK REFUND.*

WORKOUT #1

DIRECTIONS:

(1) Strap on fraction safety helmet.
(2) Adjust safety goggles over eyes.
(3) Use brain to solve problems.

1. $\frac{2}{3}$ x $\frac{3}{4}$ = _____

2. $\frac{2}{3}$ ÷ $\frac{2}{5}$ = _____

3. $\frac{3}{4}$ x $\frac{8}{9}$ = _____

4. $\frac{3}{5}$ x $2\frac{1}{2}$ = _____

5. $6\frac{2}{3}$ ÷ $1\frac{1}{9}$ = _____

6. $3\frac{2}{3}$ x $\frac{3}{22}$ = _____

7. $\frac{5}{6}$ ÷ 10 = _____

8. 12 x $2\frac{2}{3}$ = _____

9. 16 ÷ $2\frac{2}{5}$ = _____

10. $4\frac{3}{4}$ ÷ $1\frac{1}{4}$ = _____

11. $\frac{7}{8}$ ÷ $1\frac{3}{4}$ = _____

12. $8\frac{1}{6}$ x $3\frac{3}{7}$ = _____

13. $5\frac{5}{9}$ ÷ $1\frac{7}{18}$ = _____

14. $1\frac{1}{39}$ ÷ $1\frac{2}{13}$ = _____

15. $1\frac{11}{25}$ x $1\frac{13}{27}$ = _____

Wasn't that great?

Well, goodbye everyone! See you next time.

Say Ra-a-a ee-urk, Steve.

RA-A-AH! EE-E-URK!

Name _____

Ultra-Workout 3

Live from Hollywood, I'm Debbie Slash. And this is...Ultra-Workout 3! Starring, in alphabetical order:

- **The Cheese Man**
- **The Dull Guys**
- **Jerry Fragment**
- **Vickie Ganoosh**
- **Lon Largely**
- **Pokey**

And of course, me, Debbie Slash. And so, without further ado, I give you...

Ultra-Workout 3!

1. Hi, I'm Jerry Fragment, movie mogul and producer. When I'm not making multi-million dollar movie deals, I like to do problems like this one. **Find $\frac{1}{4}$ of 36. Go ahead and try it. And hey, let's do lunch soon!** _____

2. Hello, I'm the Cheese Man, star of the blockbuster *Cheese Man: The Movie.* Our movie had a budget of $40 million. Two-fifths of the budget went to mega-star Vickie Ganoosh. **How much money was Vickie paid?** _____

3. Hi, we're the Dull Guys, stars of *The Dull Guys.* You know, when we're not acting in blockbuster Hollywood mega-hits, we like to unwind by doing problems like this: **Find the product of $\frac{3}{11} \times \frac{2}{7}$.** _____

4. Hey, I'm Vickie Ganoosh, one of the stars of *Cheese Man: The Movie.* One of the most exciting moments in the movie was when a giant cheese slicer cut off $\frac{7}{8}$ of a huge block of cheese weighing $\frac{16}{21}$ ton. **How big a block did the cheese slicer cut?** _____

5. Hey there, movie star Lon Largely here. Bet you didn't recognize me without my movie make-up! But here's one thing you will recognize—a great problem: **Find the quotient of $\frac{2}{3} \div \frac{3}{4}$.** _____

6. Howdy. Pokey here, Lon Largely's co-star in *Mystery on the Fraction Express.* Our movie lasted $2\frac{1}{4}$ hours. **How long did it take to show $\frac{5}{6}$ of the movie?** _____

7. Hi, it's the Cheese Man again. Did I tell you that the screenplay for *Cheese Man: The Movie.* was inspired by a famous photograph called "Underground Velveeta"? The photograph measures $6\frac{1}{4}$ inches by $3\frac{1}{5}$ inches. **What is the area of the photograph?** _____

That's about all the time we have. So long from the greatest Workout of them all...

Ultra-Workout 3!

Name _____

The Critics

Studies show that movie critics use the same words over and over again. This list shows the top 10 words used in positive reviews. It also shows the *probability* of each word appearing in a review. For example, the probability of the word *wild* apearing is $\frac{3}{7}$. That means it is likely to appear in three out of every seven reviews.

Top 10 Positive Review Words	
wild	$\frac{3}{7}$
weird	$\frac{7}{18}$
classic	$\frac{10}{27}$
riot	$\frac{3}{11}$
blast	$\frac{2}{5}$
action-packed	$\frac{5}{12}$
side-splitting	$\frac{3}{10}$
rip-snorting	$\frac{2}{9}$
roller coaster ride	$\frac{1}{6}$
knock-down, drag-out	$\frac{2}{7}$

example, the probability that a movie will be called a "side-splitting action-packed blast" is:

$$\frac{3}{10} \times \frac{5}{12} \times \frac{2}{5} = \frac{30}{600} = \frac{1}{20}$$

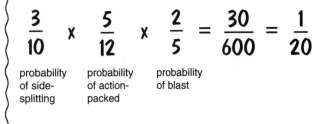

probability of side-splitting   probability of action-packed   probability of blast

Probabilities are independent of each other. So to find the probability of more than one positive word appearing in a review, you need to multiply the probabilities of each word. For

What is the probability that the movie *Let Them Eat Soup* will be called:

1.wild? _____

2. a wild roller coaster ride? _____

**3. rip-snorting
and side-splitting?** _____

**4. a rip-snorting,
side-splitting riot?** _____

What is the probability that *The President's Soup Is Cold* will be called:

5. a blast? _____

6. an action-packed blast? _____

**7. a knock-down, drag-out,
action-packed blast?** _____

**8. a side-splitting,
knock-down, drag-out,
action-packed blast?** _____

Top 10 Negative Review Words	
cheap	$\frac{5}{18}$
lame	$\frac{3}{8}$
pointless	$\frac{3}{25}$
stupid	$\frac{4}{15}$
icky	$\frac{5}{12}$
cheesy	$\frac{8}{25}$
crummy	$\frac{1}{6}$
turkey	$\frac{5}{32}$
rip-off	$\frac{2}{5}$
third-rate rubbish	$\frac{3}{16}$

What is the probability that the movie *Waiter, There's an Aardvark in My Soup* will be called:

9. a rip-off? _____

10. a cheap rip-off? _____

11. a stupid turkey? _____

**12. a pointless,
icky turkey?** _____

What is the probability that the movie *The Chicken Noodle Man* will be called:

**13. stupid,
third-rate rubbish?** _____

**14. stupid,
icky, and crummy?** _____

**15. cheesy,
third-rate rubbish?** _____

**16. icky, stupid,
third-rate rubbish?** _____

BONUS QUESTION: Which is most likely to appear in a review: rip-off, side-splitting, or stupid? How can you tell?

_____

_____

_____

_____

_____

Name _____

Arnold Guck: Man or Myth?

PART 1: BEGINNINGS

"He was a messy child," says Vivian Guck, Arnold Guck's mother. "He ate messy, he drank messy. All he did was make messes."

At age five, Guck made mud pies. He mixed 3 scoops of mud with 9 scoops of gravel and 12 scoops of water.

At age 20, Guck got a job at a toothpaste company. Soon after that, he created Tar-Gum Toothpaste. The toothpaste contained 4 parts baking soda, 6 parts black licorice gum, and 8 parts Extra Hot Garlic Salsa.

Tar-Gum Toothpaste was not a success.

"It smelled like garlic and turned your teeth black," Guck explained.

Guck was soon fired from the toothpaste company. He came home a broken man. Slowly, Guck began to admit that he had only one true talent in the world: to make disgusting things. And to be able to compare one disgusting ingredient to another, he'd have to learn how to use ratios. For example, the ratio of baking soda to salsa in Tar-Gum toothpaste was 4 parts baking soda to every 8 parts salsa.

WRITING RATIOS

ONE WAY TO DO IT

How can you write the ratio 4 to 8 mathematically?

1. Write it with words:

$$4 \text{ to } 8$$

2. Write it with a colon.

$$4{:}8$$

3. Write it so it looks like a fraction.

$$\frac{4}{8}$$

4. Simplify, if possible.

$$4 \text{ to } 8 = 1 \text{ to } 2$$

$$4{:}8 = 1{:}2$$

$$\frac{4}{8} = \frac{1}{2}$$

1. The ratio of mud to gravel in Guck's mud pies was 3 to 9. Write this ratio three different ways.

_____ _____ _____

2. Write the ratio in simplest form. _____

3. The ratio of gravel to mud was 9 to 3. Write the ratio in simplest form. _____

4. What is the ratio of water to mud in Guck's mud pies? Write the ratio using the word *to*. Make sure it's in simplest form. _____

5. What is the ratio of baking soda to black licorice gum in Tar-Gum toothpaste? Write the ratio as a fraction. Make sure it's in simplest form. _____

6. What is the ratio of salsa to baking soda in Tar-Gum? Write the ratio with a colon. Put it in simplest form. _____

7. What is the ratio of salsa to black licorice gum in Tar-Gum? Write the ratio any way you want, as long as it's in simplest form. _____

PART 2: THE LOST CAT

For a while, Guck gave up his work. Then one day his cat got lost. To lure it back, Guck mixed 12 milliliters of vinegar with 8 milliliters of rotten fish juice. The result was a powerfully bad-smelling concoction. Within an hour, it attracted not only Guck's cat, but a half dozen other garbage-loving cats and dogs in the neighborhood.

It also attracted me. I'm Warren Vuss, a scout for Wow! Inc. We're the world's leading maker of plastic puddles, fake garbage, and other such products.

"Young man," I told him, "I'm gonna make you rich!"

"You are?" Guck said.

The rest, as they say, is history. Guck's first big success for Wow! Inc. was called Fabulous Guck. To make Fabulous Guck, he mixed 3 ounces of gunk with 6 ounces of sludge and 8 ounces of muck.

The result was a greasy, grimy mess. It made you feel sick just to look at it. Touching it made your skin crawl. But that wasn't all. Fabulous Guck had the most nauseating smell I'd ever come across. And I've been in this business 35 years.

Needless to say, kids loved it. It outsold the other top-selling slime product by a 2 to 1 ratio. In other words, stores sold two Fabulous Gucks for every one of the other top-selling slime.

In simplest form, what is the ratio of...

8. ...vinegar to rotten fish juice in Guck's cat mixture? _____

9. ...gunk to sludge in Fabulous Guck? _____

10. ...sludge to muck in Fabulous Guck? _____

11. A store sold 10 cases of the other top-selling slime product. How many cases of Fabulous Guck would you expect it to sell? (Remember: FG outsold the other top-selling slime product 2 to 1.) _____

12. Suppose 40,000 cases of the other top-selling slime product were sold last year. How many cases of Fabulous Guck were sold? _____

PART 3: THE MAN WITH THE GOLDEN TOUCH

From there, Guck had one hit product after another. First there was Fabulous Guck. Then Plutz. Then Yellow Yetch. Then came Guck's biggest hit of all: Totally Gross Guck. This was the greatest product I've ever sold. It was disgusting. It was revolting. But it was also great fun.

Totally Gross Guck outsold other ooze products by wide margins. It outsold Ooze-Juice by a 4 to 1 ratio.

It outsold Crudd by 5 to 2.

Before long, both Arnold Guck and I were voted into the Disgusting Products Hall of Fame. I'll never forget the induction ceremony. I spoke first. Then Guck got up and started talking. All of a sudden, someone dumped a huge vat of Totally Gross Guck over his head.

For a moment, Guck was speechless. His head was covered with the stuff. His suit was ruined. Then he started to laugh. We all laughed. It was a great moment in the history of disgusting things.

13. A store sold 20 boxes of Ooze-Juice in one week. How many boxes of Totally Gross Guck would you expect that it sold? _____

14. A store sold 25 boxes of Totally Gross Guck in one week. How many boxes of Crudd would you expect that it sold? _____

15. A store sold 20,000 boxes of Totally Gross Guck in a year. How many boxes of Ooze-Juice would you expect that it sold in that time? How many boxes of Crudd? _____

_____

Name

Enid the Magnificent, Part 1

Hugo was twelve when his father took him to the circus. He saw the strong man, the dancing bear, the clowns, and so on. But the part he liked best was Enid the Magnificent.

"Velcome!" she said, as they entered her dark and mysterious tent. "I am Enid the Magnificent. I can change any decimal number to a fraction. Any number at all!"

The audience laughed. In those days, people never changed decimal numbers to fractions. It just wasn't done.

"How about 0.7," a man cried. "Let's see you change that to a fraction, Enid the Magnificent!"

"The number 0.7 as a fraction is $\frac{7}{10}$," Enid said coolly. A hush came over the room.

"How did she do that?" Hugo asked his father.

"I don't know," Hugo's father gulped.

Enid went on to change many decimal numbers to fractions. Can you duplicate this astounding feat? Here's how:

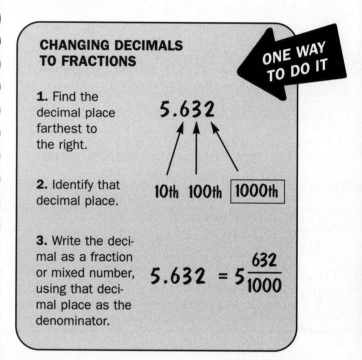

CHANGING DECIMALS TO FRACTIONS

ONE WAY TO DO IT

1. Find the decimal place farthest to the right.

5.632

2. Identify that decimal place.

10th 100th 1000th

3. Write the decimal as a fraction or mixed number, using that decimal place as the denominator.

$5.632 = 5\frac{632}{1000}$

Now you try it. Write each decimal number as a fraction or mixed number.

1. 3.2 = _____

2. 0.4 = _____

3. 5.89 = _____

4. 64.8 = _____

5. 0.05 = _____

6. 24.09 = _____

7. 0.004 = _____

8. 13.001 = _____

9. 562.029 = _____

10. 37.040 = _____

After that, things got very strange indeed. People kept shouting numbers. And Enid kept changing them to fractions.

"It's a trick!" cried one man. "I want my money back!"

But it wasn't a trick. Enid did it again and again. Finally, a woman said, "Let's see you change $\frac{3}{10}$ to a decimal!"

"A fraction to a decimal!" someone shouted. "That's impossible!"

"SILENCE!" replied Enid the Magnificent.

Then, calm as can be, Enid turned the fraction $\frac{3}{10}$ into 0.3.

The place exploded into an uproar. Once again, Enid had done the impossible. She had changed a fraction to a decimal. You can do it, too. Here's how:

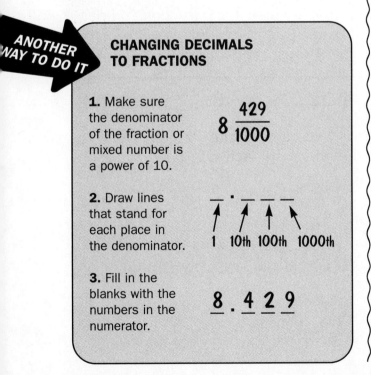

CHANGING DECIMALS TO FRACTIONS

1. Make sure the denominator of the fraction or mixed number is a power of 10.

$$8\frac{429}{1000}$$

2. Draw lines that stand for each place in the denominator.

$$\_\ .\ \_\ \_\ \_$$
1   10th 100th 1000th

3. Fill in the blanks with the numbers in the numerator.

$$8\ .\ 4\ 2\ 9$$

Can you write these fractions as decimals?

11. $\frac{9}{10}$ = _____ 16. $6\frac{341}{1000}$ = _____

12. $\frac{7}{10}$ = _____ 17. $\frac{7}{100}$ = _____

13. $\frac{23}{100}$ = _____ 18. $4\frac{8}{100}$ = _____

14. $2\frac{5}{10}$ = _____ 19. $\frac{3}{1000}$ = _____

15. $1\frac{25}{100}$ = _____ 20. $2\frac{37}{1000}$ = _____

Through all this, Hugo's father sat quietly. He was a stern man. He had known few pleasures in life, but fractions were one of them. Hugo's father loved fractions. But he also believed in right and wrong. And he'd always thought it was wrong to change one kind of number to another.

But now he wasn't so sure.

"Your tricks are good," Hugo's father said to Enid.

"They are not tricks," replied Enid.

"Change $\frac{3}{8}$ to a decimal," he said calmly.

The whole room gasped. To our left, one man actually fainted and had to be carried away. To change a fraction like $\frac{3}{8}$ — a fraction with a denominator that WASN'T a power of 10—to a decimal was—well, at that time, it was just unthinkable.

Could Enid the Magnificent do it? Find out the thrilling conclusion of this story on page 70 in Enid the Magnificent, Part 2.

Name _____

Enid the Magnificent, Part 2: Enid Does the Unthinkable

Hugo, a young boy, had just witnessed an amazing display of fractional power (see page 68). Was Enid the Magnificent for real? Could she really do things with numbers that no one else could do? Or was her power just a trick?

Hugo would find out when his father gave Enid the Magnificent the ultimate challenge—to change the fraction $\frac{3}{8}$ to a decimal. Could it be done?

Enid calmly announced the answer: "The fraction $\frac{3}{8}$ is equal to 0.375."

No one in the room could believe it. There was shouting. There was stomping. People from the audience demanded that Enid explain how she had done what she had done.

Can you write these fractions as decimals? (Round repeating decimals to the nearest thousandth.)

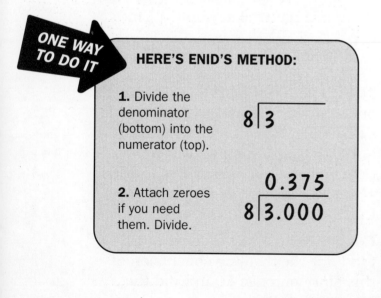

ONE WAY TO DO IT

HERE'S ENID'S METHOD:

1. Divide the denominator (bottom) into the numerator (top).

$$8\overline{)3}$$

2. Attach zeroes if you need them. Divide.

$$8\overline{)3.000} = 0.375$$

1. $\frac{1}{2}$ = _____

2. $\frac{2}{5}$ = _____

3. $\frac{3}{4}$ = _____

4. $\frac{4}{5}$ = _____

5. $\frac{2}{9}$ = _____

6. $\frac{3}{8}$ = _____

7. $\frac{5}{8}$ = _____

8. $\frac{2}{7}$ = _____

9. $\frac{7}{11}$ = _____

10. $\frac{19}{20}$ = _____

Hugo remembers little after that. People shouted. The goons in the audience grew louder and louder. Finally, they rushed the stage. The tent started to fall.

Suddenly, all was in darkness.

Hugo found himself outside in a ditch. He looked up to see frightened eyes. It was Enid the Magnificent.

"There she is!" cried one of the goons.

"Quick," said Hugo's father. "Come with us."

They escaped to a small inn at the edge of the woods. Hugo's father gave Enid a cup of steaming hot tea.

"Drink this," he said.

"You saved my life," Enid said.

"Perhaps," Hugo's father said. "Has such a thing ever happened to you before?"

"Too often," Enid said. "These people, they don't understand fractions."

"Neither did I," Hugo's father said. "You opened my eyes tonight, Enid."

She smiled. "I must go," she said.

"But wait," Hugo's father said. "There is so much you have to teach us."

"You know enough already," Enid said. "What you don't know, you can discover on your own."

"But how can we ever thank you?" Hugo's father asked.

"You've thanked me enough already," Enid said.

Then she walked out the door and was gone. Hugo and his father never saw her or heard about her again. But on the table, she left a piece of paper with these problems on it.

Write the fractions as decimals and the decimals as fractions. (Round repeating decimals to the nearest thousandth.)

11. $\frac{13}{100}$ = _____

12. $\frac{1}{5}$ = _____

13. .76 _____

14. 8.08 = _____

15. $\frac{4}{9}$ = _____

16. $9\frac{3}{10}$ = _____

17. 77.08 = _____

18. 678.009 = _____

19. $\frac{12}{15}$ = _____

20. $\frac{4}{7}$ = _____

Name _____

Name That Fraction

CONNIE: And now it's time for NAME THAT FRACTION. I'm your host, Connie Twinkle. Here's our All-Star Panel: Gunther Duff, Jane Pesto, and Mickey Toothache. Hello, Panel! *(wild applause)*

PANEL: Hi, Connie!

CONNIE: And now it's time to introduce our Secret Fraction. Tell us about yourself, Secret Fraction.

(even wilder applause. Secret Fraction enters in disguise.)

FRACTION: Hello, Panel. Hey, what can I tell ya? I'm a common fraction. You've probably seen me around — in pizzas, hockey games, candy bars, stuff like that. *(audience murmurs)*

GUNTHER: I know it's early but I'm gonna make a guess here. Are you $\frac{5}{6}$?

BUZZER: B-u-u-u-z-z!

CONNIE: I'm sorry, Gunther. The Secret Fraction is much smaller than $\frac{5}{6}$. We move to Jane Pesto.

JANE: Are you larger than $\frac{1}{4}$ and smaller than $\frac{1}{2}$?

FRACTION: Yes I am.

JANE: Hmm. I think I saw you at a party once. Is your numerator odd or even?

FRACTION: It's odd, Jane. Very odd. (Audience roars with laughter.)

1. Name 2 fractions that are smaller than $\frac{5}{6}$. _____ _____

2. Name 2 fractions larger than $\frac{1}{4}$ and smaller than $\frac{1}{2}$. _____ _____

3. Name a fraction smaller than $\frac{1}{2}$ that has an odd numerator. _____

JANE: I'm going to guess...$\frac{3}{8}$?

BUZZER: B-u-u-u-z-z!

CONNIE: I'm sorry, Jane, that's too big. We'll move to Mickey Toothache.

MICKEY: You sound familiar to me. If I split you in half, would you be much bigger than $\frac{1}{6}$?

FRACTION: Not a bit. But please don't split me in half. I'll go on a diet. I promise! (Audience howls)

MICKEY: I think I know who it is, Connie. Are you $\frac{1}{3}$?

BUZZER: Ding! Ding! Ding!

CONNIE Very well done, Mickey. Secret Fraction, will you please come out! (Fraction takes off disguise)

GUNTHER: (smacks his forehead) I should've known!

JANE: Well aren't you cute.

FRACTION: I try to be. (Audience chortles.)

MICKEY: Can I ask you one question. As a decimal, what do you look like?

FRACTION: As a decimal, my real name is too long to pronounce. Most people call me 0.33 for short.

MICKEY: Of course.

CONNIE: And now it's time to move on to our Super Secret Bonus Fraction round. (Super Secret Fraction enters. Big applause.)

BONUS FRACTION: I come from a family of large denominators. But I wanted to be in show biz, so I changed my denominator to 8 when I left home. At that time I was so skinny, I had a numerator of 1. But then I started working out and doubled my numerator size.

MICKEY: My goodness!

4. Name a fraction that's smaller than $\frac{3}{8}$ and larger than $\frac{1}{4}$. _____

5. What fraction could you split in half to get $\frac{1}{6}$? _____

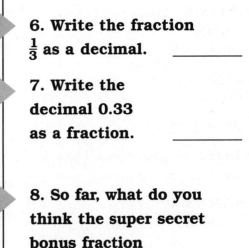

6. Write the fraction $\frac{1}{3}$ as a decimal. _____

7. Write the decimal 0.33 as a fraction. _____

8. So far, what do you think the super secret bonus fraction could be? _____

BONUS FRACTION: That's just the beginning. It was around then that people started noticing me. I got a job as a model. Then I started getting really big. My denominator stayed the same, but my numerator size increased to 6.

MICKEY: Wait. Are you $\frac{6}{13}$?

BUZZER: B-u-u-u-z-z!

BONUS FRACTION: No I'm not. Around at that time I starting writing myself in simplest form. It was unbelievable! I was the same size, only I now had a different numerator and denominator.

JANE: This is fascinating. It must be wonderful to be a fraction.

BONUS FRACTION: Oh it's okay. But you never really feel WHOLE, you know?

(Audience hoots with laughter.)

But anyway, at this time, I added myself to $\frac{1}{8}$ and became the fraction I am today.

CONNIE: Well, panel, there you have it— today's Super Secret Fraction's story. Now it's time for each of you to record your guesses on your cards.

GUNTHER: Oh goodness, Connie. This is really a toughie.

MICKEY: Yeah, Connie. Can't you give us a little hint?

CONNIE: I'd love to, Mickey. But as you know, it just wouldn't be Name That Fraction if I gave you clues. Good luck, panel, and good night.

▶ **9. Write the fraction.** _____

▶ **10. Write the fraction in simplest form.** _____

▶ **11. Add $\frac{1}{8}$ to your answer for problem 9. Write the Super Secret Fraction in lowest terms.** _____

▶ **12. What is the decimal value of the Super Secret number?** _____

Name _____

Martha's Brain Game

I'm Martha Crunch, your personal fractions trainer.

And this is Steve.

RA-A-AH! EE-E-URK!

Guess what?

We found a great new game you can play using my brain!

Martha's Brain Game

Actually, it uses my IMAGINATION. That's the part of my brain that's full of good things.

Here's how you play.

1. You need a penny, the brain board at right, and paper and pencil. The object of the game is to score the most points.

2. Spin the penny on the board. Watch where it lands. Then think of an example that fits that category.

• **Example 1**: The penny lands on Funny Stuff. You have to think of something funny.

3. The other players rate your funny idea. Ratings must be between 1 and 100, with 100 as the best score.

4. Multiply the rating by the fraction next to the category. The number you get is your score.

• **Example 2:** Your funny idea gets a rating of 20. You then multiply 20 x $\frac{2}{5}$ to get a score of 8.

• **Example 3:** The penny lands on Daydreams. Your daydream gets a rating of 18. You multiply 18 x $\frac{1}{4}$ to get a score of $4\frac{1}{2}$.

5. Write your scores on separate paper. Scores count only if you multiply correctly.

6. Add up the scores. The first player to get 100 points wins.

I just know you're going to have a lot of fun with my Brain Game.

And who knows. It may even improve your own brain!

So long everyone!

Martha's Imagination
(Not drawn to scale)

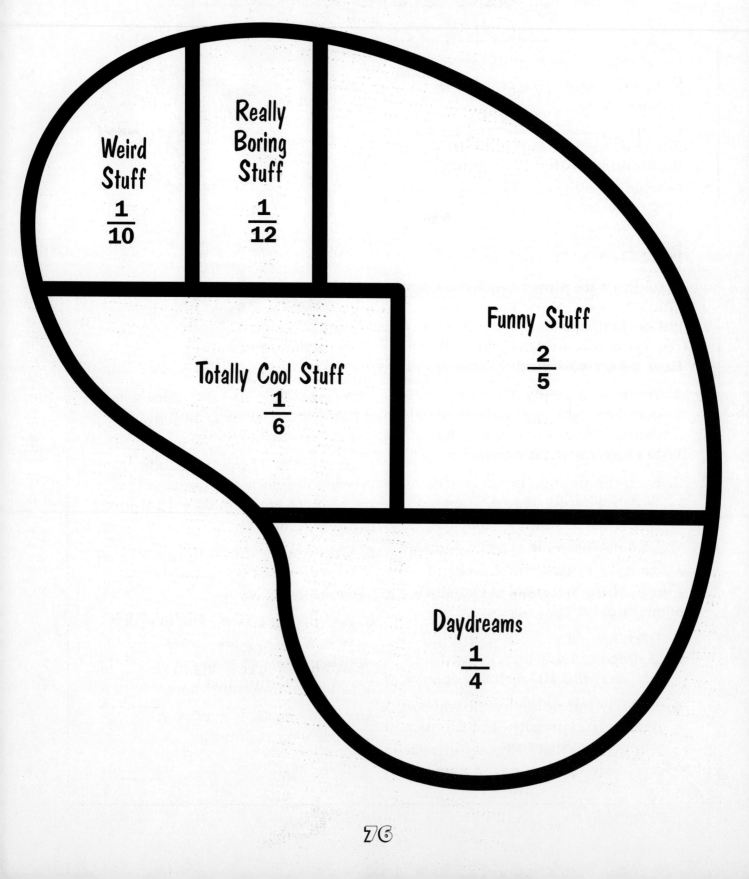

Weird Stuff
$\frac{1}{10}$

Really Boring Stuff
$\frac{1}{12}$

Funny Stuff
$\frac{2}{5}$

Totally Cool Stuff
$\frac{1}{6}$

Daydreams
$\frac{1}{4}$

Name _____

The Ultimate Fraction Workout, Part 1

Hi. Martha Crunch here, your personal fractions trainer.

Now that you know all there is to know about fractions, it's time you learned soming about me......Martha Crunch.

So without further ado, here I am...

THE MARTHA CRUNCH STORY

PART 1 — THE EARLY YEARS

1. I was born at a very young age. When I was $\frac{1}{2}$ year old, I found my first true love in life—fractions. My mother claims I was actually $\frac{3}{5}$ of a year old at the time. **When was I older—at $\frac{1}{2}$ year or $\frac{3}{5}$ year?** _____

2. As an infant, I loved to play with my food. I remember one time I had $\frac{2}{3}$ of a bowl of mush. I changed it into a fraction that was still equal to $\frac{2}{3}$. **Write two different fractions I might have used.** _____ _____

3. I used to cry and scream when fractions weren't written in simplest form. Here are some fractions: $\frac{18}{42}$, $\frac{16}{25}$, $\frac{28}{63}$. **Which ones made me cry and scream?** _____ _____

4. Rewrite the fractions that made me cry and scream so they ARE in simplest form. _____ _____

5. As a toddler, I became obsessed with improper fractions. When I was $2\frac{3}{4}$ years old I expressed my age as an improper fraction. **How many years old did I say I was?** _____

6. At age $\frac{30}{7}$ I started becoming interested in mixed numbers. **What was my age as a mixed number?** _____

7. In kindergarten I met Steve, my bird. He was doing jumping jacks in his cage at the pet store. He did them for $2\frac{7}{8}$ minutes. Then he stopped and did sit-ups for $3\frac{5}{8}$ minutes. **How many minutes did he exercise in all?** _____

8. I noticed that Steve did sit-ups for longer than jumping jacks. **How many minutes longer did he do sit-ups?** _____

9. I took Steve home with me. It was then I realized he could talk. He said, "Please mix $\frac{3}{4}$ ounces of mango juice and $\frac{1}{6}$ ounce of papaya juice in my water tray." **What was the total weight of the juice?** _____

10. Steve drank $\frac{1}{2}$ ounce of the juice. **How much was left over?** _____

11. It turned out that Steve loved fractions. One of the first things he ever asked me was, **"What is $4\frac{5}{7} + 1\frac{1}{14}$?"** _____

I worked out the answer. But Steve's curiosity about fractions was unending. He kept asking me questions like these:

12. What is $6\frac{7}{10} + 3\frac{1}{6}$? _____

13. What is $8\frac{1}{3} - 2\frac{1}{4}$? _____

14. What is $13\frac{1}{5} - 7\frac{3}{5}$? _____

15. What is $4\frac{7}{12} + 9 + \frac{5}{9}$? _____

16. And finally, what is $20\frac{2}{3} - 10\frac{5}{6}$? _____

17. I was exhausted. Before I met Steve I remember I weighed 60 pounds. Before long, I'd lost $6\frac{2}{3}$ pounds. **How much did I weigh then?** _____

It soon dawned on me that if I liked doing fractions so much I should get paid for them. So I put out a sign that said: I'LL DO FRACTIONS FOR YOU—25¢

But nobody came. And now we were out of money. Would Steve and I ever get paid for doing fractions? All I can tell you is that this story...

WILL BE CONTINUED.

IF YOU WANT TO FIND OUT WHAT HAPPENED, SEE THE ULTIMATE FRACTION WORKOUT, PART 2 ON PAGE 79.

Name _____

The Ultimate Fraction Workout, Part 2

Hi. Martha Crunch here, your personal fractions trainer. And this is the second part of The Martha Crunch Story.

I call it...

THE MARTHA CRUNCH STORY, PART 2

THE YEARS THAT FOLLOWED PART 1

1. As you'll recall, I'd put out a sign that said I'LL DO FRACTIONS FOR YOU—25¢. But nobody came. So I put up another sign. It said, I'LL DO FRACTIONS FOR YOU—$\frac{1}{5}$ OFF THE REGULAR 25¢ PRICE. **How many cents off the regular price was this?** _____

2. Steve and I were down to our last 18¢. I spent $\frac{2}{3}$ of that on some birdseed. **How much did it cost?** _____

3. I spent what remained of our 18¢ on a piece of bread. **How much did the bread cost?** _____

4. Then it hit me: musical fractions. I found an old guitar. I multiplied $\frac{5}{8}$ x $\frac{12}{25}$ to the tune of "Yankee Doodle Dandy." **What answer did I get?** _____

5. I tried musical division. I divided $\frac{5}{7}$ by 10 to the tune of "Swanee River." **What answer did I get?** _____

6. I multiplied $4\frac{1}{5}$ x $\frac{5}{14}$ to the tune of "Happy Birthday to You." **What answer did I get?** _____

7. I tried dividing $10\frac{1}{2}$ by $1\frac{2}{5}$ to the tune of "Twinkle Twinkle Little Star." **What answer did I get?** _____

8. Steve and I had no money left. Everyone seemed to love our music. But no one was interested in paying money for it. Luckily, we found $\frac{1}{2}$ of a pizza. We sold $\frac{3}{4}$ of that half for two dollars. **What fraction of an entire pie did we sell?** _____

9. I used the money to buy more pizza. I bought $\frac{6}{7}$ of a whole pizza. I divided it into 3 parts. **What fraction of the entire pie was each piece?** _____

10. I kept buying pizza and selling it for a little more than I paid for it. I did this for $3\frac{1}{2}$ weeks. For $\frac{2}{3}$ of that time, I was selling anchovy pizza. **For how many weeks did I sell anchovy pizza?** _____

11. Then I got a new idea: an aerobic fractions video. It would be $2\frac{1}{2}$ hours long. I would divide it into 5 equal parts. **How many hours would each part last?** _____

12. I shortened the video to only 60 minutes. Commercials took up 12 of those minutes. **What fraction of the video did commercials take up?** _____

13. People complained that the video had too many commercials. I cut all but 3 commercials. Each lasted $1\frac{2}{3}$ minutes. **How many minutes did the commercials take up now?** _____

14. What fraction of the entire HOUR did the commercials now take up? _____

15. Then it happened. The famous adventurer Texarkana Bernstein bought my video. She liked it and started telling her friends about it. Sales took off. Suddenly, I was famous.

I'll never forget the first thing Tex asked me. "Can you change $\frac{27}{100}$ to a decimal?" she said. Of course I could! **What did I write?** _____

16. I did a Holiday Fractions Special for National TV. On it I changed 0.3 to a fraction. **What answer did I get?** _____

17. One thing led to another. Steve and I became Fraction Specialists for all the big Hollywood stars. Did you see the movie *Dull and Duller*? I did the fractions for that movie. I wrote 0.6 as a fraction in simplest form. **What answer did I get?** _____

18. In another movie, *Cheese Man 4: Major Meltdown*, I wrote $\frac{7}{8}$ as a decimal. **What answer did I get?** _____

19. Pretty soon I became a personal fractions trainer for the rich and famous. I once explained to zillionaire cracker mogul Victor Kronski how to put $\frac{7}{10}$, $\frac{3}{4}$, 0.73, and $\frac{71}{100}$ in order from greatest to least. **Can you put them in order?** _____ _____ _____ _____

20. Don't get me wrong. I loved working for the rich and famous, but it bothered me that I couldn't help REGULAR folks like you and me. So when they offered me the job to be the personal fractions trainer here, I jumped at the chance. I still work for the rich and famous 2 days a week. The other 4 days I work here. **What's the ratio of the days I work for the rich and famous to the days I work here? Write the ratio in simplest form.** _____

So that's pretty much my story.

I LOVE being a personal fractions trainer. I really do. Because it lets me help people like you.

But you don't really need my help anymore. As far as fractions go, you're an ACE.

So I guess it's time to be moving along. So long, everyone.

Keep in touch!

Answers

Martha Crunch, Personal Fractions Trainer
SKILL: 1

1. $\frac{2}{3}$

2. $\frac{1}{2}$

3. $\frac{3}{5}$

4. $\frac{3}{7}$

5. $\frac{4}{5}$

6. $\frac{1}{8}$

7. $\frac{5}{9}$

8. $\frac{7}{10}$

9. $\frac{6}{11}$

10. $\frac{4}{4}$

Great Artists of the World Draw Fractions
SKILL: 2

1. $\frac{3}{7}$

2. $\frac{4}{7}$

3. $\frac{2}{7}$

4. $\frac{5}{7}$

5. $\frac{4}{8}$ or $\frac{1}{2}$

6. $\frac{4}{8}$ or $\frac{1}{2}$

7. $\frac{5}{8}$

8. $\frac{8}{8}$ or 1

9. $\frac{3}{4}$

10. $\frac{1}{4}$

11. $\frac{3}{8}$

12. $\frac{5}{8}$

13. $\frac{3}{12}$ or $\frac{1}{4}$

14. $\frac{9}{12}$ or $\frac{3}{4}$

15. $\frac{6}{12}$ or $\frac{1}{2}$

16. $\frac{6}{12}$ or $\frac{1}{2}$

17. $\frac{2}{3}$

18. $\frac{1}{3}$

19. $\frac{1}{4}$

20. $\frac{3}{4}$

Try This: Answers will vary.

The History of Fractions
SKILL: 3

1. $\frac{1}{2}$ of the large pie should be colored in

2. $\frac{2}{3}$ of the small pie should be colored in

3. $\frac{3}{4}$ of the long board should be colored in

4. $\frac{1}{4}$ of the short board should be colored in

5. 5 sheep

6. 4 coins

7. Drawing should be divided into 5 parts; 3 parts should be colored.

8. Drawing should be divided into 10 parts; 7 parts should be colored.

9. 3 shapes should be colored.

10. 8 shapes should be colored.

Dear Fraction Lady
SKILL: 4

1. $\frac{2}{3}$ is greater, Randy's Candy Bar

2. $\frac{7}{8}$ is greater, Lloyd's worse

3. $\frac{3}{8}$ is greater, get the haircut

4. In order: $\frac{7}{8}, \frac{3}{4}, \frac{2}{3}, \frac{1}{7}$

Louie Lewis, Fractional Private Eye
SKILL: 5

1. Students should show that diagrams, models, or cut-outs of $\frac{1}{2}$ and $\frac{2}{4}$ are equivalent. They might also show a way that 1 is half of 2.

2. Students should show that diagrams, models, or cut-outs of $\frac{1}{2}$ and $\frac{4}{8}$ are equivalent. They might also show that 4 is half of 8 in the same way that 1 is half of 2.

3. Explanations should indicate that the fractions take up the same part of the total but are divided into different numbers of parts.

4. Sample response: $\frac{5}{10}$

5. Sample response: $\frac{6}{12}$

6. Sample response: $\frac{7}{14}$

7. Sample response: $\frac{10}{20}$

8. Sample response: $\frac{2}{6}$

9. Sample response: $\frac{3}{9}$

10. Sample response: $\frac{5}{15}$

11. Sample response: $\frac{10}{30}$

12. Sample responses: $\frac{6}{9}$, $\frac{10}{15}$

13. Sample response: $\frac{9}{12}$, $\frac{15}{20}$

14. Sample responses: $\frac{4}{10}$, $\frac{8}{20}$

15. Sample responses: $\frac{2}{12}$, $\frac{6}{36}$

Martha and Steve:
Simplest Form
SKILL: 6

1. $\frac{1}{2}$

2. $\frac{3}{7}$

3. $\frac{1}{5}$

4. $\frac{2}{7}$

5. $\frac{3}{5}$

6. $\frac{3}{7}$

7. $\frac{1}{4}$

8. $\frac{2}{5}$

9. $\frac{5}{6}$

10. $\frac{4}{5}$

11. $\frac{1}{2}$

12. $\frac{6}{7}$

13. $\frac{4}{5}$ 14. $\frac{4}{7}$

15. $\frac{2}{3}$

16. $\frac{8}{9}$

17. $\frac{3}{4}$

18. $\frac{2}{5}$

19. $\frac{9}{10}$

20. $\frac{2}{3}$

Joe Trella, Fraction Fella
SKILL: 7

1. $1\frac{1}{2}$

2. $1\frac{2}{3}$

3. $1\frac{3}{4}$

4. $4\frac{1}{2}$

5. $2\frac{4}{5}$

6. $3\frac{1}{5}$

7. $3\frac{1}{8}$

8. $5\frac{5}{6}$

9. $5\frac{7}{10}$

10. $6\frac{1}{15}$

11. $1\frac{1}{3}$

12. $1\frac{1}{2}$

13. 4

14. $2\frac{1}{3}$

15. $2\frac{1}{2}$

16. $1\frac{6}{7}$

17. $1\frac{1}{4}$

18. $1\frac{1}{4}$

19. $4\frac{1}{6}$

20. $5\frac{1}{2}$

21. $\frac{3}{2}$

22. $\frac{8}{3}$

23. $\frac{17}{5}$

24. $\frac{9}{2}$

25. $\frac{21}{8}$

26. $\frac{29}{6}$

27. $\frac{31}{3}$

28. $\frac{59}{7}$

29. $\frac{73}{6}$

30. $\frac{122}{3}$

Never More, Baltimore!
SKILL: 8

1. $\frac{3}{4}$

2. $8\frac{2}{3}$

3. OK

4. $\frac{5}{6}$

5. $14\frac{3}{4}$

6. $\frac{3}{5}$

7. OK

8. $\frac{2}{5}$

9. $\frac{2}{3}$

10. $\frac{6}{7}$

11. $\frac{3}{16}$

12. $12\frac{7}{8}$

13. $5\frac{1}{5}$

14. OK

15. $7\frac{2}{3}$

16. $\frac{2}{3}$

Ultra-Workout 1
QUIZ 1

1. $\frac{3}{8}$

2. Answers will vary.

3. $\frac{1}{3}, \frac{1}{2}, \frac{3}{5}, \frac{7}{10}, \frac{7}{8}$

4. Answers will vary.
Sample response: $\frac{4}{10}, \frac{6}{15}$

5. $\frac{3}{4}$

6. $1\frac{3}{4}$

7. $\frac{14}{3}$

Rex Roper's Believe It or Not!
SKILL: 9

1. $1\frac{2}{7}$ hour

2. $\frac{3}{7}$ hour

3. $1\frac{4}{5}$ ounces

4. 1 ounce

5. $1\frac{1}{5}$ ounce

6. $\frac{2}{5}$ oz

7. $\frac{1}{4}$

8. $\frac{3}{4}$

9. $\frac{15}{16}$

10. 1

11. $\frac{1}{2}$ pound

12. $\frac{1}{3}$ pound

13. $\frac{1}{2}$ pound

14. 2 pounds

15. $\frac{2}{5}$

16. $\frac{1}{3}$

17. $\frac{2}{3}$

18. $\frac{7}{15}$

Texarkana Bernstein: Episode 1
SKILL: 10

1. $29\frac{1}{4}$ inches

2. $\frac{3}{4}$ inch

3. $15\frac{3}{8}$ inches

4. Answers will vary

5. $20\frac{1}{2}$ inches

6. $6\frac{3}{4}$ inches

7. $9\frac{1}{2}$ inches

8. No, their hat sizes don't add up to 30 inches.

9. It has to be larger because Stinky's hat size is less than half of 30 inches.

10. No, because the sum of $14\frac{5}{8}$ and $13\frac{3}{8}$ is 28 inches, not 30 inches.

11. $16\frac{5}{8}$ inches

12. 30 inches

13. $3\frac{1}{4}$ inches

14. 2 inches

15. It must be the sheriff. He's the only one in town who has the right hat size.

Meg O'Malley of the Fraction Police
SKILL: 11

1. $\frac{3}{4}$

2. $\frac{7}{10}$

3. $\frac{5}{6}$

4. $\frac{14}{15}$

5. $\frac{7}{8}$

6. $\frac{11}{12}$

7. $\frac{9}{14}$

8. $\frac{3}{5}$

9. $\frac{19}{24}$

10. $\frac{5}{6}$

Martha's Brain
SKILL: 12

1. Stubborn Determination

2. Old Pasta Recipes

3. Gumption; $\frac{1}{24}$

4. Stubborn Determination; $\frac{1}{4}$

5. $\frac{3}{4}$

6. $\frac{1}{4}$

7. Stubborn Determination and Gumption

8. Gumption, Old Pasta Recipes, Vim & Vigor

9. Vim & Vigor

Texarkana Bernstein: Episode 2
SKILL: 13

1. $5\frac{5}{6}$

2. $4\frac{11}{12}$

3. $8\frac{5}{12}$

4. $9\frac{7}{12}$

5. $10\frac{3}{4}$

6. $14\frac{1}{4}$

7. $15\frac{5}{12}$

8. $13\frac{1}{3}$

9. $14\frac{1}{2}$

10. 18

11. $28\frac{3}{4}$

12. 25

13. 17 and 44

14. 18, 25, 43

Billy Doogan, Roving Weather Man
SKILL: 14

1. $5\frac{1}{2}$ degrees

2. $13\frac{1}{4}$ degrees

3. $7\frac{3}{4}$ degrees

4. $14\frac{1}{3}$ degrees

5. $1\frac{1}{3}$ degrees

6. $\frac{1}{4}$ degree

7. $8\frac{3}{4}$ inches

8. $1\frac{1}{4}$ degrees

9. $2\frac{1}{2}$ degrees

10. $3\frac{3}{4}$ degrees

11. $1\frac{1}{3}$ miles per hour

12. $4\frac{1}{3}$ inches

13. $7\frac{2}{3}$ inches

Ultra-Workout, Too!
QUIZ 2

1. $\frac{11}{15}$

2. $1\frac{1}{6}$ pounds

3. $\frac{11}{18}$

4. $\frac{23}{24}$ cup

5. $3\frac{3}{10}$

6. $1\frac{1}{3}$ blocks

7. $13\frac{11}{24}$

8. $8\frac{13}{20}$ gallons

Emily Taproot
SKILL: 15

1. 45

2. 24

3. 27

4. 7, 9

5. 24

6. 11

7. 56

8. 14

The Frackie Awards
SKILL: 16

1. $\frac{1}{3}$

2. $\frac{1}{2}$

3. $\frac{7}{10}$

4. $\frac{5}{8}$

5. $\frac{3}{8}$

6. $\frac{1}{2}$

7. $\frac{2}{5}$

8. $\frac{1}{3}$

9. $\frac{5}{8}$

10. $\frac{1}{10}$

11. $\frac{1}{5}$

12. 12 seconds

Emily Taproot's Winky-Tinky Tiggiesworth
SKILL: 17

1. 1

2. $\frac{1}{2}$

3. $\frac{1}{50}$

4. $\frac{8}{3}$ or $2\frac{2}{3}$

5. $\frac{18}{7}$ or $2\frac{4}{7}$

6. $\frac{9}{4}$ or $2\frac{1}{4}$

7. $\frac{3}{5}$

8. $\frac{8}{1}$ or 8

9. $\frac{33}{4}$ or $8\frac{1}{4}$

10. $\frac{2}{5}$

11. $\frac{4}{3}$ or $1\frac{1}{3}$

12. $\frac{50}{50}$ or 1

13. $\frac{3}{2}$ or $1\frac{1}{2}$

14. $\frac{2}{3}$

15. $\frac{7}{5}$ or $1\frac{2}{5}$

16. $\frac{5}{7}$

17. The reciprocal of a reciprocal is the original number itself.

Louie Lewis, The Case of the Flipping Fractions
SKILL: 18

1. $1\frac{1}{2}$

2. 2

3. $3\frac{1}{3}$

4. $2\frac{1}{2}$

5. $10\frac{1}{2}$

6. $1\frac{1}{3}$

7. $1\frac{1}{2}$

8. 9

9. 16

10. $\frac{5}{12}$

11. $\frac{14}{15}$

12. $2\frac{3}{4}$

13. $3\frac{1}{3}$

14. $\frac{4}{7}$

15. $\frac{5}{9}$

Officer Meg O'Malley: Episode 2
SKILL: 19

1. 2

2. $2\frac{1}{3}$

3. $6\frac{1}{4}$

4. $10\frac{1}{2}$

5. 8

6. $2\frac{1}{5}$

7. $2\frac{2}{9}$

8. $1\frac{2}{3}$

9. $9\frac{1}{3}$

10. $5\frac{5}{6}$

11. 2

12. $\frac{3}{20}$

Yucky Cooking With Mr. Pierre
SKILL: 20

1. 5 ounces

2. $1\frac{1}{4}$ ounces

3. 3 ounces

4. 6 servings

5. $2\frac{1}{2}$ pounds

6. $\frac{3}{8}$ pound

7. 5 pieces

8. 3 pieces

9. $2\frac{11}{12}$ ounces

10. $\frac{7}{12}$ ounce

11. 7 portions

12. $\frac{5}{24}$ ounce

Martha's Video Workout
SKILL: 21

1. $\frac{1}{2}$

2. $1\frac{2}{3}$

3. $\frac{2}{3}$

4. $1\frac{1}{2}$

5. 6

6. $\frac{1}{2}$

7. $\frac{1}{12}$

8. 32

9. $6\frac{2}{3}$

10. $3\frac{4}{5}$

11. $\frac{1}{2}$

12. 28

13. 4

14. $\frac{8}{9}$

15. $2\frac{2}{15}$

Ultra-Workout 3
QUIZ 3

1. 9

2. $16 million

3. $\frac{6}{77}$

4. $\frac{2}{3}$ ton

5. $\frac{8}{9}$

6. $1\frac{7}{8}$ hour

7. 20 square inches

The Critics
SKILL: 22

1. $\frac{3}{7}$

2. $\frac{1}{14}$

3. $\frac{1}{15}$

4. $\frac{1}{55}$

5. $\frac{2}{5}$

6. $\frac{1}{6}$

7. $\frac{1}{21}$

8. $\frac{1}{70}$

9. $\frac{2}{5}$

10. $\frac{1}{9}$

11. $\frac{1}{24}$

12. $\frac{1}{128}$

13. $\frac{1}{20}$

14. $\frac{1}{54}$

15. $\frac{3}{50}$

16. $\frac{1}{48}$

BONUS QUESTION: Icky, because it has the largest probability. It will appear in almost half of all negative reviews.

Arnold Guck
SKILL: 23

1. 3 to 9, 3:9, $\frac{3}{9}$

2. 1 to 3, 1:3, or $\frac{1}{3}$

3. 3 to 1, 3:1, or $\frac{3}{1}$

4. 4 to 1

5. $\frac{2}{3}$

6. 2:1

7. 4 to 3, 4:3, or $\frac{4}{3}$

8. 3 to 2, 3:2, or $\frac{3}{2}$

9. 1 to 2, 1:2, or $\frac{1}{2}$

10. 3 to 4, 3:4, or $\frac{3}{4}$

11. 20 cases

12. 80,000 cases

13. 80 boxes

14. 10 boxes

15. 5,000; 8,000

Enid the Magnificent, Part 1
SKILL: 24

1. $3\frac{2}{10}$

2. $\frac{4}{10}$

3. $5\frac{89}{100}$

4. $64\frac{8}{10}$

5. $\frac{5}{100}$

6. $24\frac{9}{100}$

7. $\frac{4}{1000}$

8. $13\frac{1}{1000}$

9. $562\frac{29}{1000}$

10. $37\frac{40}{1000}$

11. 0.9

12. 0.7

13. 0.23

14. 2.5

15. 1.25

16. 6.341

17. 0.07

18. 4.08

19. 0.003

20. 2.037

Enid the Magnificent, Part 2
SKILL: 25

1. 0.5

2. 0.4

3. 0.75

4. 0.8

5. 0.222

6. 0.375

7. 0.625

8. 0.286

9. 0.636

10. 0.95

11. 0.13

12. 0.2

13. $\frac{76}{100}$

14. $8\frac{8}{100}$

15. 0.444

16. 9.3

17. $77\frac{8}{100}$

18. $678\frac{9}{1000}$

19. 0.8

20. 0.571

Name That Fraction!
SKILL: 26

1. Answers will vary. Sample response: $\frac{1}{2}$, $\frac{1}{4}$

2. Answers will vary. Sample response: $\frac{3}{8}$, $\frac{1}{3}$

3. Answers will vary. Sample response: $\frac{3}{7}$

4. Answers will vary. Sample response: $\frac{1}{3}$

5. $\frac{1}{3}$

6. .33

7. $\frac{33}{100}$

8. $\frac{2}{8}$

9. $\frac{6}{8}$

10. $\frac{3}{4}$

11. $\frac{7}{8}$

12. 0.875

Test 1

1. $\frac{3}{5}$ year

2. Answers will vary. Sample response: $\frac{4}{6}$, $\frac{8}{12}$

3. $\frac{18}{42}$ and $\frac{28}{63}$

4. $\frac{18}{42} = \frac{3}{7}$, $\quad \frac{28}{63} = \frac{4}{9}$

5. $\frac{11}{4}$ years

6. $4\frac{2}{7}$ years

7. $6\frac{1}{2}$ minutes

8. $\frac{3}{4}$ minute

9. $\frac{11}{12}$ ounces

10. $\frac{5}{12}$

11. $5\frac{11}{14}$

12. $9\frac{4}{5}$

13. $6\frac{1}{12}$

14. $5\frac{3}{5}$

15. $14\frac{5}{36}$

16. $9\frac{5}{6}$

17. $53\frac{1}{3}$ pounds

Test 2

1. 5¢

2. 12¢

3. 6¢

4. $\frac{3}{10}$

5. $\frac{1}{14}$

6. $1\frac{1}{2}$

7. $7\frac{1}{2}$

8. $\frac{3}{8}$ pie

9. $\frac{2}{7}$ pie

10. $2\frac{1}{3}$ weeks

11. $\frac{1}{2}$ hour

12. $\frac{1}{5}$

13. 5 minutes

14. $\frac{1}{12}$

15. 0.27

16. $\frac{3}{10}$

17. $\frac{3}{5}$

18. 0.875

19. $\frac{3}{4}$, 0.73, $\frac{71}{100}$, $\frac{7}{10}$

20. 1 to 2; 1:2; $\frac{1}{2}$